THE
NUMBER PLATE
BOOK

by John Harrison

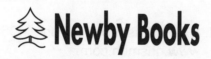

First published 2019

© John Harrison 2019

Front cover designed by Caroline Haley

TH 3 would have been issued by Carmarthen County Council in July 1929.
NUM 83R sold for £2,500 at a DVLA Auction in February 2006.
P1 ATE sold for £4,000 at a DVLA Auction in June 1999.
800 K was never actually issued as a trade plate, only as a normal issue, but we trust you will accept our artistic licence. It is possible that 800 E and 800 W were issued as trade plates.

Newby Books
Easingwold Town Hall Company Ltd
The Advertiser Office
Market Place
Easingwold
York   YO61 3AB

Tel 01347 821 329
www.newbybooks.co.uk

ISBN

Printed by G H Smith & Son, Easingwold, York, YO61 EAB
Tel 01347 821 329.   www.ghsmith.com

CONTENTS

INTRODUCTION

You might consider that vehicle registration is a very minor part of motoring history, but can you imagine the chaos that would exist on our roads if vehicles were not registered. I have the sort of mind that finds this aspect of motoring history absolutely fascinating. I have tried to communicate this interest in this book in a way that is easy to understand, presenting a basic history of the United Kingdom registration system from 1903 to date. Some aspects of the registration system are quite complicated to explain and whether I have achieved this objective I will leave you, the reader, to decide. I do hope you will find this book interesting and a fun read, whether you are already well versed in how the number plate system works or totally new to the topic.

Although my name is on the front cover, this book would not have been produced without the help of a lot of people involved in the registration hobby. In the hobby we share a lot of information as many discoveries are the result of observing and then literally comparing notes. Quite a few hobbyists have helped me with specific queries I have needed the answers to in writing this book. I would not propose to name all as so many have helped and I might inadvertently miss somebody out. A lot of hobbyists have provided photos for the book and these are duly acknowledged underneath the photos with thanks. I would like to thank Adrian Tranmer and Colin Spong for proofreading and Caroline Haley for producing the front cover and Richard Beswick-Arthur for help with the back cover. I would also like to thank the staff of various libraries who have enabled me to use their facilities and their helpful staff, namely the British Library, the National Archives and the Royal Automobile Club Library.

CHAPTER 1 – THE INTRODUCTION OF REGISTRATIONS

A 1 was London's first number, not the first to be issued in Britain, and was issued to Earl Russell, though the story that he queued all night to obtain it may not be true. This is an early car that bore this number. Martin McLaughlin.

BE was issued by Lincolnshire Lindsey from December 1903. This is a 1908 Austin 100hp Grand Prix Car. Europlate.

Motorists today take the requirement to display a registration plate for granted and would not consider this to be an infringement of their civil liberties, but if you read early 20th century newspapers or motoring magazines you will see that frequently people expressed concern that cars should have to be numbered.

Concern was also expressed that motorists were being required to carry registrations, but horse-drawn vehicles or cycles were not. It must be remembered that at this time motor cars were not very much faster than horse-drawn vehicles. Nowadays horses have all but disappeared from our roads, so nobody expects them to carry registrations, though the debate as to whether cyclists should have to carry number plates continues to this day.

The Motor Car Act 1903 introduced vehicle registration in the United Kingdom. The Act not only dealt with the registration of vehicles, but also other issues arising from the introduction of the then new-fangled motor car such as road signs and speed limits. Britain was slow to introduce registrations compared with other countries and this seems to have been the consequence of the civil liberties lobby opposing them. In deciding when the first number plates were adopted, one has difficulty defining what comprises a number plate as they might have been displayed on the dashboard rather than "publicly" and they may have not been allocated by the authorities but rather chosen by the owner like boat owners choose their boats' names. As far as can be verified, the first "conventional" plates were issued by Baden, Germany in 1896 and in 1899 the Netherlands started what appears to be the first national system.

The format adopted for early British plates was one or two letters followed by up to four numerals. The original intention was for there to be a maximum of three numerals, but it was soon clear that the growth in vehicle ownership would necessitate four. The letters indicated the local authority that issued the registration. Codes containing G, S and V were reserved for use in Scotland and those

M 661 was issued in 1904 to a 8-10hp Humber by Cheshire. This photo shows that hyphens were often used to separate the letters and numbers when registrations were first issued.

containing I or Z for Ireland. Codes containing Q were not used, no doubt to avoid possible confusion with O. Codes were allocated by the Local Government Boards. England and Wales shared a board – Wales was given no special treatment in terms of code allocation. County Councils and County Boroughs in England and Wales were responsible for issuing registrations and each one was given a one-or two-letter code. These codes were allocated by population size, starting with A for London, the authority with the biggest population, B for Lancashire, C for Yorkshire West Riding through to Y for Somerset, then AA for the County of Southampton (which was then the official name for what we now know as Hampshire) through to FP for Rutland, the smallest authority by population size.

Many early plates had a hyphen between the letters and numerals. The specimen diagrams of plates in the Motor Car (Registration and Licensing) Order 1903 showed a hyphen but this was not referred to in the text of the Order. Nevertheless, one was frequently used when plates were introduced, but the practice gradually died out.

Codes with "G", "S" and "V" in them were reserved for use in Scotland. TS was allotted to Dundee and TS 1 was Dundee's first issue when plates were introduced. The original vehicle bearing TS 1 was scrapped in 1922. In 1927 the City applied for and obtained special permission from the Ministry of Transport to reissue TS 1 for use on the Provost's car and it has been used on the Provost's car ever since. Europlate

In Scotland, County Councils and Burghs with over 50,000 population were responsible for issuing registrations. The three largest authorities were given the single-letter codes; Glasgow (G), Edinburgh (S) and Lanarkshire (V). The remaining codes were allocated in alphabetical order with the County Councils coming first and then the Burghs. Ireland was not, of course, partitioned until 1922, so the codes containing I and Z were used both north and south of what is now the border. County Councils and County Boroughs were responsible for issuing registrations. I and Z were not used as single letters initially, though Dublin County Council subsequently started using Z in 1926. The two-letter codes were allocated in alphabetical order as in Scotland, with the sequence having the County Councils followed by the County Boroughs. Letter pairs containing G, S or V and I or Z were not used in Ireland. It should be noted when looking at more modern code lists some authorities have changed names which could cause confusion. Elginshire (SO) in Scotland became Morayshire and more predictability, after partition in Ireland, Kings County (IR) became Offaly and Queens County (CI) became Laoighis (now referred to as Laois). It should also be noted that in what was the Irish Free State and what is now known as the Republic of Ireland the registration system remained based on the British one until 1986. After partition, when Northern Ireland needed new codes, they used those ending in Z and the Republic used those beginning with Z.

When considering vehicle registrations, censorship is inevitably an issue that arises. Certain codes were omitted from the sequence; DD, DT and ER, plus CS, FS, GS, SF and SG in Scotland. DD was considered to stand for "drop dead", but was given to Gloucestershire when it needed another code in 1921. DT stood for "delirium tremens", but when Doncaster became a separate county borough in 1927 it was logical that it should be given this mnemonic code. ER was the royal cypher, but in 1921 when Cambridgeshire required

The letter H was allotted to Middlesex and H 6460 is a preserved 1910 Panhard et Levassor London taxicab. Note the contemporary Public Carriage Office licence plate. This style of plate, usually referred to as a "Lion and Unicorn plate", was used up to the Second World War.

another code this was no longer the case, so it was issued to that authority. It is not clear the Scottish codes were omitted; the most likely explanation I have heard is at this time number plates were frequently hand painted and there was the possibility of confusion with between Cs and Gs and Es and Fs.

Two authorities were not happy with the codes they were given. Dorset was given BF and at that time it was considered to stand for "bloody fool" and Northampton DF which was considered to stand for "damned fool". Both authorities complained and were issued with new codes. Dorset was given FX which was the next available code in the alphabetical sequence (I will explain what this means in the next chapter) and Northampton a mnemonic NH. Any marks issued with BF and DF codes were subsequently withdrawn. When Gloucestershire needed a second code in 1924 it was given DF and presumably its residents did not protest too much (they already had had DD inflicted on them, of course). BF was only used again in 1960 when Staffordshire was running short of marks to issue, but it could only be used in three-letter combinations. More recently, however, BFs have been used for pre-1930 age-related re-registrations, i.e. marks given to vehicles imported second-hand or replacement marks given when a vehicle has its original number transferred off, and some have also been sold in DVLA (Driver and Vehicle Licensing Authority) auctions.

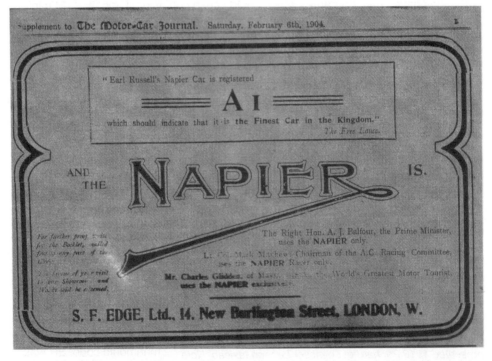

The fact that a make of car bore a particular number might not be the obvious selling point for it, but this is how the Napier was advertised in "The Motor-Car Journal" of 6 February 1904.

It is frequently reported that the first British registration was A 1 which was issued to Earl Russell and he queued all night to obtain it. The first statement is certainly incorrect and the second one is probably false too. Registrations had to be displayed on motor vehicles used on public roads on or after 1 January 1904 and generally local authorities started issuing numbers before that date. Many started in December 1903 with 18 December being a common commencement date. At least three started in November 1903; Buckinghamshire (date of commencement not known), Hastings (23 November) and Somerset (25 November). "Motoring Illustrated" on 19 December 1903 stated that London did not start issuing marks till 7 December 1903, so A 1 clearly was not the first mark issued. From surviving records the first registration issued in Britain seems to have been Hastings' DY 1. It should be noted that the original vehicle bearing DY 1 was scrapped, but the Borough resurrected the number as a £5 reissue (this is explained in the chapter dealing with personal plates) for its mayoral car. Like many local authorities at a time when most local authorities have very tight budgets, Hastings has now sold its mayoral registration to raise much needed funds. Instead of DY 1, the number that was previously on the deputy mayor's car, a very appropriate DY 1066, is now being used on the mayor's car. Moving onto the issue whether Earl Russell queued all night to obtain A 1, there is no contemporary record in "The Car Illustrated" or elsewhere that he did so, so we cannot be sure this actually happened.

When registrations were first issued, numbers were often reissued when a vehicle

was scrapped or exported. Also, it was a common practice for motorists to keep their registration and transfer it from vehicle to vehicle when they bought a new car. Thus registration was a "fluid" process and it was not the norm for a vehicle to have the same number for life. Frequently motorists would register their cars with a particular authority, so they could have a number with their initials or for other reasons. At this time motorists could register their vehicles with any authority, not necessarily their own authority. There are many examples of vehicles being

Dennis Brothers, the Guildford-based vehicle manufacturers, sometimes registered their products in Stockport so they could get DB numbers for them. DB 61 is such an example. This photo comes from "The Automotor Journal" of 10 March 1906.

registered with other authorities for special reasons. For example, although the Dennis Brothers Company which then made both cars and lorries was based in Guildford, their vehicles were sometimes registered in Stockport so they could get DB marks and similarly some Harrods delivery vans were registered in Renfrew so they could get HS numbers. Similarly in 1909 Christabel Pankhurst registered a 15hp Austin landaulet at Leith and received the mark WS 95.She presumably chose Leith so she could get a "WS" mark, the "WS" no doubt standing for "Women's Suffrage". Inspection of early local authority registers reveals other examples of such "personalised" numbers.

The Motor Car Act initially covered vehicles of up to 3 tons. "Heavy locomotives" were separately covered by the Locomotives Act 1898. Agricultural locomotives, locomotives not used for haulage purposes and locomotives belonging to road authorities used entirely within their areas were registered under the Act and all other heavy locomotives were licensed under it. Heavy locomotives, whether registered or licensed, carried a small numbered plaque issued by the relevant county council; the difference between the plaques on registered and licensed locomotives being that licensed vehicles plaques carried the date of licensing. The Heavy Motor Car Order of 1904 changed the upper weight limit for a motor car from 3 to 5 tons. This Order also required local authorities to keep a separate register of heavy motor cars, vehicles over 2 tons.

Norfolk was an authority that used lead zeros for its registrations in its "heavy motor car" series. AH 0775 was issued to a Burrell steamroller by Norfolk in 1920.

As well as being required to keep a separate register of heavy motor cars, authorities could keep separate registers for cars and motorcycles if they chose to. Thus, some authorities differentiated between different vehicle types, usually by either having different blocks of numbers for different types or having odd numbers for motorcycles and even ones for other vehicles or vice versa. Some duplicated numbers for different vehicle types and three authorities, namely Hanley (later merging into Stoke-on-Trent) (EH), Oldham (BU) and York (DN), even had three series for the three vehicle types so each number could potentially be issued in triplicate. Some authorities used lead zeroes in front of the number on the plates of heavy motor cars, namely Bath (FB), Berkshire (BL), Buckinghamshire (BH), Clackmannan (SL), Isle of Ely (EB), Norfolk (AH) and West Sussex (BP). Like Hanley/Stoke-on-Trent, Oldham and York, Norfolk had three separate series for cars, motorcycles and heavy motor cars, but the latter series used lead zeroes, so there was only duplication, not triplication. In 1921 Merioneth (FF) issued a lead zero series for motorcycles from FF 01 to FF 0112, the only example of lead zeroes being used for something other than heavy motor cars. Some vehicles survive with their zero prefixes, but others have lost them. Uniquely and for reasons which are not apparent Aberdeen Burgh used an "X" prefix for its heavy motor car series, i.e. plates were in an RS-X 123 format, the series reaching RS-X 152 before being abandoned. These practices ceased when the Roads Act 1920 came into effect on 1 January 1921, some continued beyond that date. As we shall see in Chapter 3, however, Staffordshire (E, RE and RF) continued segregation of motorcycles until 1947 and Eastbourne (HC and JK), which had initially given motorcycles even numbers and other vehicles odd ones, continued segregation until 1948.

CHAPTER 2 – THE SYSTEM DEVELOPS

THE NEW NUMBER-PLATE.

AN interesting epoch in the development of automobilism is marked by the fact that 10,000 motor vehicles have now been registered in London. Since our last issue the Local Government Board has promulgated an official order to the effect that the letters " LC " have been awarded to the London County Council as a distinguishing mark in lieu of the letter " A " which has hitherto done duty. Clearly this decision was made

LONDON'S NEW NUMBER-PLATE.

none too soon, for, as the accompanying illustration shows, the Council has already entered upon its second series. The numbers LC 1 to 29 have been retained by the Council for its Works Department, and the first number issued to an applicant from the general public is LC 30, which is now affixed to the Decauville belonging to Mr. R. Moffatt Ford.

How "The Car Illustrated" reported the introduction of London's second code, LC, on 3 May 1905. London was the first local authority to require a second code.

The three Local Government Boards only issued a few of their available codes in 1903, one to each authority, and gradually more and more codes were allotted. The first call on new codes was the creation of new county boroughs in England and Wales in October 1904 when the next two marks in the alphabetical sequence, FR and FT (FS was reserved for use in Scotland, of course as it contained the letter "S"), were given to Blackpool and Tynemouth respectively when they became separate county boroughs. FU was then omitted (I will leave readers to work out why!), though Lindsey subsequently was allotted it in 1921. FV was reserved for use in Scotland as it contained the letter "V". FW was kept back for no obvious reason. As explained in the previous chapter FX was issued to Dorset in place of BF. Then, when Southport was created a

county borough in October 1905, it received the code FY.

It would not be practical to list all subsequent code allocations. As well as codes for new county boroughs, new codes were needed for local authorities that were exhausting their original code, i.e. approaching 9999. London was the first authority to need a second code and in 1905 A 9999 was followed by LC 1, LC being a mnemonic for London County. This was followed by another mnemonic, LN in 1906, then LB, LD and LA, then the remaining L* codes in alphabetical order, omitting LG, LI, LJ, LS, LV and LZ. These were generally reserved for use in Scotland and Ireland, of course, but LJ was not used as after the 1903 allocation most codes containing "J" were initially held back for some reason. Middlesex was the second authority to need another code and in 1912 it started using the mnemonic MX.

When Southend-on-Sea was created as a separate county borough on 1 April 1914 it was given the next available code HJ. HJ 11 would, of course, have been a very early issue by that authority. In case you are having difficulty spotting HJ 11's number plate, it is immediately below the front windscreen. The charabanc is a Daimler. The other charabanc (make unknown) is J 6345. J was issued by Durham from December 1903 to November 1922. – Lynn Haseldine Jones.

Basically three principles were applied in allotting subsequent codes to local authorities:

1. Sometimes the next available code in alphabetical sequence was used. We have already seen how the codes from FR to FY were issued and this pattern continued as further new county boroughs were created; HA to Smethwick in April 1907, HB to Merthyr Tydfil in April 1908, HC to Eastbourne in April 1911 and so on.
2. Blocks of sequential letters were kept for larger authorities. We have already noted how London had most L* codes. Similarly, it was subsequently given most X* and Y* combinations and many of the G* ones. Incidentally, as might be anticipated, London was by far the largest registration authority. Ultimately, it had 73 two-letter codes, plus the single-letter one, A. Many other examples of such blocks could be cited. For example, Middlesex had many M* combination, Birmingham had most of the O* combinations, plus O itself and Liverpool whose original code was K subsequently had KA to KD, plus KF (KE was issued to Kent as it was a mnemonic for that authority).
3. Mnemonics/initials were used. London's LC and LN, Middlesex's MX, Northampton's NH, Kent's KE and Doncaster's DT have already been referred

to. Other examples were (Kingston upon) Hull's KH, Liverpool's LV, Reading's RD and the West Riding of Yorkshire's WR. Though Buckinghamshire's BH and Bolton's BN might appear similarly mnemonic, their receiving these codes in the 1903 allocation was purely coincidental as marks were issued alphabetically based on the authority's population. Similarly Northumberland receiving NL appears to have been the result of them being

Durham started its second series, UP, in July 1927 and UP 110 would have been issued shortly thereafter. – Roy Yallop (whose grandparents are on the motorcycle)

given the next available code (principle 1 on the previous page), rather than it being a deliberate mnemonic issue. An example of an initial code is Kent receiving ten K* codes and we will consider further examples shortly.

In Scotland and Ireland subsequent code allocations were generally based on principles 1 and 2.

With combinations containing G, S and V reserved for it, Scotland proved to be over-provided with codes and from 1928 onwards codes containing G and V started to be issued south of the border (S remained exclusively Scottish). Also, as has been mentioned, apart from the initial 1903 allocation, very few codes containing J had been used and these were also now issued. Many of these G, J and V issues incorporated the first letter of the relevant authority, namely Berkshire (JB), Birkenhead (BG), Blackpool (BV), Caernarvonshire (JC), Cornwall (CV), Essex (EV), Hertfordshire (JH), Isle of Ely (JE), Norfolk (NG), Northamptonshire (NV), Oxford (JO), Wiltshire (WV) and Wolverhampton (JW). Though not strictly a mnemonic or phonetic, it is appropriate to mention VT being issued by Stoke-on-Trent as its second code as it stood for the five towns that comprised the borough.

Although codes containing G, S and V were reserved for use in Scotland, the powers that be managed to produce one exception. In 1930 Dundee was allotted YJ, even though some codes containing G were given to English authorities at the same time. By 1932, the only codes now remaining unused were BF, OO and WC, plus MN which has been withheld to avoid possible confusion with Manx registrations.

Quite a few new county boroughs were created in the early years of the twentieth century and given new codes. There were other changes to local government governance which affected code allocation. In 1910 the county borough of Stoke-on-Trent was formed by merging Hanley with Burslem, Fenton, Longton, Stoke and Tunstall. In 1915 Devonport (DR) was absorbed into Plymouth. In Scotland, Glasgow absorbed the burghs of Govan (US) and Partick (YS) in 1912 and Edinburgh absorbed the burgh of Leith (WS) in 1920. Stoke continued to issue Hanley's EH code (in three separate series for cars, motorcycles and heavy motor cars, of course). Plymouth started using Devonport's DR code, starting from the point where Devonport had ceased, when its originally code CO reached 9999 in 1926. Edinburgh and Glasgow were allotted and used other codes before using the unused numbers with the codes of their "absorbed" local authorities. This difference in behaviour is probably the result of Plymouth's codes being dealt with by the English and Welsh Local Government Board and the Scottish authorities by the Scottish Local Government Board

Though it may not be very clear on this photo, the number of this car is US 66. Govan issued US 1 to 529 before the authority was absorbed by Glasgow on 1 November 1912. This photo appeared on the cover of "The Cyclecar" on 28 February 1913. The car is a Dew Monocar. As it sports a relatively low number, 66, we can presume this was not the first vehicle to carry this number. The building behind is thought to be Battle Abbey. The business of Harold Dew who developed the car was based at nearby Eynsford, Kent at this time.

practices. The burghs of Motherwell and Wishaw were merged in 1921 to form one burgh which had a population over 50,000, the minimum population for a Scottish burgh to become a registration authority, so it required a code and was given GM.

Mention needs to be made in relation to certain two-letter series which were not used as normal series. Between 1926 and 1934 Middlesex issued MM and MU to Stewart and Ardern, the biggest distributors of Morris cars in the London area. Middlesex's MG is another interesting series. When we look at military vehicle registrations, we shall see from 1921 to 1939 the

University Motors put many "MG" numbers onto MG cars. This photo, taken from a Dutch magazine, shows Amy Johnson being presented with an MG six-cylinder car, a gift from Sir William Morris (later Lord Nuffield) after she successfully flew solo from London to Australia in 1930. Europlate

War Department registered their vehicles at Middlesex. MG 8001 to 9999 was a block reserved for military registrations. A large proportion of the remainder of the series was issued to University Motors who distributed MG cars. Thus many ended up on MGs, though by no means all as University Motors did supply other makes of cars. As a consequence of this special arrangement, the first MG marks were issued in 1930 and the series was not completed until 19 years later in 1949. University Motors subsequently received blocks in UMG, UML (University Motors Ltd) and YMG. Finally, in terms of special series, RE should be mentioned. The reason for this will be explained more fully in the next chapter, but Staffordshire used this combination exclusively for motorcycles.

London was allotted 74 letter pairs in addition to its single-letter code "A". GW was its 70th letter pair commenced in December 1931. GW 2658 was issued to a Talbot Six. – Graham Wilkins.

The Roads Act 1920 came into effect on 1 January 1921. This saw the introduction of the tax disc and the log book. Before 1921 one could register one's vehicle with any local authority one wished, but now it had to be registered with the authority in which it was normally kept, except that businesses could register their vehicles in their principle place of business if a vehicle was not normally kept in one area. This did not necessarily mean that a vehicle would have a number plate with a local code, but rather that the local authority where the vehicle was registered would have a record of the whereabouts of the relevant documentation. Thus, for example, if a vehicle had an Essex number but it was kept in Hertfordshire, Hertfordshire would keep the file. Essex would, however, be notified that Hertfordshire had the documentation so if the police or anybody else wanted to know who the registered keeper was, they could be traced. Under the Road Vehicles (Registration and

Licensing) Regulations 1924 it became possible to register a new previously unregistered vehicle with the authority in whose area it was purchased.

Before 1921, as has been explained, it was not unusual for cars' registrations to be changed or voided numbers to be reissued. These practices now ceased – a vehicle would keep the same number for its lifetime. Additionally, the provisions for separate registers for cars, motorcycles and heavy motor cars were dropped and generally local authorities ceased practices of having different blocks, using odd or even numbers for vehicles of different types and having duplicate or even triplicate series. Clackmannan did, however, as an exception, continue using its series for heavy motor cars with lead zeros until 1925. The registration system for heavy locomotives over 5 tons under the Locomotives Act 1898 was withdrawn and such vehicles were now registered as any other vehicle. Thus, many traction engines and steam lorries have numbers first issued in 1921 though they are in fact older. Within this context it

should also be noted that frequently the dates of first registration of pre-1921 vehicles were not properly recorded under the registration system that existed then, so often they are shown on DVLA records as being first registered in 1921.

On 1 October 1930 the size of rear number plates on motorcycles and light invalid carriages was increased from half the size of car plates to two thirds. The Ministry of Transport originally proposed that the plates should be car-sized but that was not proceeded with. Also, whereas previously motorcyclists had the option of

This photo which comes from the Dundee Evening Telegraph of 5 February 1930 shows the effect of the change in rear number plate sizes introduced during that year.

having their front or rear plates illuminated, the rear plate had to be illuminated. Although nowadays changes to vehicle legislation is not applied retrospectively, this provision applied to all motorcycles then in use.

CHAPTER 3 – ON TO THREE LETTERS

AAA 1 was Hampshire's first three-letter mark issued in December 1934. Europlate

By the early 1930s the format of one or two letters followed by up to four numerals was reaching its limits as virtually all available codes had been issued. A new format was therefore required and what was chosen was three letters followed by up to three numerals. One advantage of the new format claimed at the time was it kept plates to a maximum of six digits, so larger plates and consequently larger plate apertures on vehicles were not needed. The second and third letters were to be the local authority code preceded by a serial letter, i.e. if the authority code was BC, the progression would be ABC 1 to 999, BBC 1 to 999, etc. I, Q and Z were not to be used as initial letters. It should be noted that local authorities only switched to three-letter issues when they ran out of two-letter ones and indeed when year letters were introduced from 1963 on a few small Scottish authorities were still using the two-letter format.

Staffordshire was the first authority to issue a three-letter combination, ARF 1, in July 1932. The background to this is interesting, although complicated. Staffordshire had three codes, E, RE and RF, though obviously E could not be used in a three-letter format. Staffordshire had duplicate E series, one for motorcycles and one for all other vehicles. Staffordshire was an authority where in the early days more motorcycles were registered than other vehicles which was not unusual at this time. At the end of 1920 when the Roads Act 1920 came into effect, the motorcycle series had reached E 5042. E 5043 to 9999 was then used for cars, etc and motorcycles were registered in RE. When cars reached E 9999, RF was commenced for non-motorcycle registrations. When RF 9999 was reached, ARF 1 followed on, but motorcycles continued to be registered in RE. Cars progressed through ARF,

This AEC Regent III fire engine, CU 5705, was registered in South Shields in November 1951. Although three-letter combinations first appeared in 1932, South Shields did not start issuing them until November 1957 as it was a small authority.

BRF and CRF. When CRF was completed, DRF had not been authorised for issue, so ARE, BRE and CRE were used for non-motorcycle registrations whilst motorcycles were still registered in RE. After CRE was issued, non-motorcycle issues progressed DRE, DRF, ERE, ERF, etc. When motorcycles reached RE 9999 segregation of motorcycles ceased and a common series was used. This was in 1947 when the authority was part way through NRF. RE was the only two-letter combination used exclusively for motorcycles.

ADX 1 was Ipswich's first three-letter issue released in February 1950. Such a significant mark was not issued to any vehicle, but to Ipswich Corporation's first motor bus, an AEC Regent – previously the authority had only operated trolleybuses. Both the bus and its registration survive and are on display at the Ipswich Transport Museum. The photo also shows ADX 196. This was issued to a Sunbeam trolleybus, also operated by Ipswich Corporation, in July 1950. This too is preserved at the Ipswich Transport Museum. Stuart Ray, Ipswich Transport Museum

I have briefly referred to Staffordshire's unusual order of issue for three-letter combinations. It would, however, be helpful to consider what the normal practice was. I will take Cornwall as illustrating how most authorities progressed their issues. It had three two-letter codes, AF, CV and RL. Its three-letter issues progressed alphabetically, i.e. AAF, ACV, ARL, BAF, BCV, BRL, CAF, etc. Not all authorities adopted such an obvious sequence. Four authorities, Birkenhead, Coventry, Leicester and Northumberland used their three-letter issues in the same order as they had been issued their two-letter ones, e.g. Northumberland's two letter codes were NL, TY and JR and were issued in that order and its three-letter combinations progressed ANL, ATY, AJR, BNL, BTY, BJR, CNL, etc. Leicester abandoned this practice when it started issuing reversed combinations (If you do not understand what is meant by "reversed combinations", this is explained in the next chapter). Devon adopted a somewhat peculiar practice. Its codes in order of issue were T, TA, TT, UO, DV and OD. T could not, of course, be used in three-letter combinations. It started with ATA and BTA. One would have expected CTA to have followed, but it had not at that time been authorised for issue, so ATT and BTT followed, then AUO and BUO, then ADV and BDV, then AOD and BOD. CTA to ETA had by then been authorised, so CTA, DTA and ETA were used. It then hit another "stop" as FTA had not been authorised for issue, so CTT to ETT, etc followed up to EOD. After EOD came FTA to JTA and again a "stop" of no further combinations being authorised for issue was hit, so FTT to JTT followed and so on to JOD. At this point Devon adopted a more normal sequence from KTA onwards, except that the practice of Birkenhead, Coventry, Leicester and Northumberland was copied in that the marks followed the sequence in which the original letter pairs had been issued, i.e. KTA, KTT, KUO, KDV, KOD, LTA, etc.

There are other examples of authorities not following the normal sequence. For example, for a period Bedford and Surrey issued two series simultaneously. From 1937, commencing with DVP, Birmingham reserved special series for commercial vehicles. Subsequently reserving special series for Birmingham City Transport, the Austin Motor Export Company and the Home Delivery Export Series

This Vauxhall Velox was the author's father's first car. The L-plate was for his mother who was learning to drive. RKC was issued by Liverpool in June and July 1954

(vehicles bought tax-free for export) meant issues were not entirely alphabetical and similarly Coventry started reserving series for Home Delivery Export, so did not fully keep to the sequence explained above. The two largest authorities, London and Middlesex, also deviated from normal sequence. In London's case this was the result of the need to set aside special series for the General Post Office and government departments, plus from 1946 to 1952 special series for commercial vehicles. Middlesex was the most complex authority during this period. This is the consequence of special series being reserved for War Department vehicles up to

These two Hillman Minxes participating in the Tulip Rally have LKJ marks issued by Kent in November 1948. Europlate

1939 (we will look at the registration of military vehicles in Chapter 16), the reservation of some series for manufacturers or dealers and the segregation of commercial vehicles from 1937 and motorcycles from 1942 until reversed marks were introduced. Also, NMC to NMY were withheld – it is at the request of the Metropolitan Police – but authorised use in 1961 when the authority was running short of marks.

Reversed NMY were issued before the forward combinations. There were other authorities which did not keep to the usual alphabetical sequence for various reasons including Angus, Cheshire, Durham, Glamorganshire, Kent, West Bromwich and Wolverhampton.

Certain four-letter words are considered to be rude, but some three-letter ones are also. As I have implied above, before any three-letter combination could be issued, it had to be authorised and not all were, of course. It was definitely a case of "No SEX please, We're British," though some "SEXes" have now been sold at DVLA Auctions, such as E5 SEX, SEX 70N and, perhaps surprisingly, SEX 1E. Many other words considered potentially offensive were not authorised, such as APE, GOD, JEW, LAV and SOD. It is not just English words which have been withheld as DUW which is Welsh for God and BAS which is Gaelic for death were not allowed. Propriety has

not been the only reason for withholding combinations; USN was not used to avoid possible confusion with United States Naval registrations and London withheld XXX and YYY for possible use for a diplomatic series which never came to fruition. In chapter 1 we encountered lead zeroes being used, mainly for heavy motor cars and as a consequence AHO and BHO, but none of the other potential "confusables", were omitted. DWO was not authorised for issue, although no DW marks were issued with lead zeroes. Obviously sensibilities about what is acceptable change and some letter trios which were once withheld

CTC was issued by Lancashire from July to September 1937. The car is a MG TA Midget. Europlate.

are now offered in DVLA auctions such as APE, BAS, BOG, BUB, BUG (much to the delight of Volkswagen owners, no doubt), DAM, HOG and SOT. Conversely, WOG was issued in 1958 and with T-suffix in 1978 in error, but it is now no longer used. Thinking of errors, although APE was not authorised, it was issued normally with T-suffix by mistake.

Some three-letter series were reserved for particular users. I do not propose to list them all, but just some of the more significant or interesting ones. The Post Office was Britain's biggest vehicle user and normally their vehicles were registered in London at this time. The Post Office took many whole blocks of 999 numbers. Until 1936 the Post Office had only been given blocks of 200 or 300 numbers. Starting with CLP the Post Office was given whole series or, more accurately all but 1 to 10 of a series as these numbers were reserved for "special issues" (it is thought these were reserved for diplomats' cars or imported cars, particularly American which had smaller plate apertures, so could not accommodate a six-digit plate). Starting with GGH in December 1939, the Post Office was given the whole series from 1 to 999 – presumably as there was a war on the authority could not be bothered with fripperies like special registrations and cars were no longer being imported from America.

Interestingly, JYX and LUL comprised all Morris Z vans and SLF all Morris Minor vans (there were further one-make Post Office series in London's reversed and year-letter series). Another series was especially reserved for the Post Office, GPO. Though PO is a West Sussex code, GPO was issued by London to Post Office vehicles, GPO 1, 2 and 3 going to travelling post offices. Reversed GPO and GPO-C were also later issued by London to Post Office vehicles.

In chapter 2 we learnt that Morris distributors Stewart and Arden had all MM and MU issues. Middlesex continued this practice for some time in the three-letter era receiving initially AMU, BMU, CMU, DMU, EMU, DMM and EMM in that order. Stewart and Arden then started receiving separate series for cars, *MM numbers namely FMM, GMM, HMM, JMM, and commercials, *MU ones, namely FMU, GMU, HMU and JMU. When Stewart and Arden stopped receiving their own series Vauxhall Motors started obtaining whole series from Middlesex, namely MMU, RMU, TMU, VMC, VML, VMV, WMV and XMU. VMC and VML were, of course, mnemonics for Vauxhall Motor Company and Vauxhall Motors Ltd.

The London, Midland and Scottish Railway Company and its successor the London Midland Region of British Railways registered its vehicles in Hertfordshire and had the following exclusive series, ANK, BNK, CNK, GAR, GRO, JJH, LAR, OAR, RNK, SUR and WRO. Mention should also be made of JOJ which was exclusively used for Birmingham buses and FYS exclusively used for Glasgow buses, plus SGD which was used for Glasgow buses and other Glasgow Corporation vehicles.

All except RYE 1 to 9 were issued to London motorcycle dealer Claude Rye and issued over a two-year period from 1955 to 1957. Although a single issue rather than a whole series, AMY 1 was specially issued early by Middlesex for the aviatrix Amy Johnson. Similarly GRA 1 to 37 were issued a year early by Derbyshire to the Greyhound Racing Association.

All RYE numbers except RYE 1 to 9 were put onto motorcycles supplied by London dealer, Claude Rye. RYE 754 was issued to this 600cc Panther in November 1956. – Bernard Minton

The Second World War obviously resulted in a reduction in the number of new vehicles registered as car factories switched production to military equipment. The blackout lighting restrictions introduced on 1 September 1939 included provisions that rear number plates should no longer be illuminated. From 30 June 1945 rear number plates again had to be illuminated. Originally this requirement was to be applied from 29 March 1945, but the date was put back three months to enable vehicle owners to make the necessary alterations.

CHAPTER 4 – REVERSED ISSUES

1000 E was the first reversed registration to be issued and has been transferred off the original vehicle that bore it. This photo of it on a Vauxhall Cavalier was taken some time ago – at the time of writing the number is on a Citroen Picasso. Reg Wilson

Middlesex commenced reversed MM in January 1961. To avoid duplication with trade plates, Middlesex started some reversed two-letter series at 1000 (and many other authorities adopted the practice of starting reversed issues at a higher number than 1), but reversed MM started at 1. 33 MM was an F-Type Vauxhall Victor. Europlate

The next format for British registrations that was introduced had the numbers followed by the letters, e.g. 1234 AB or 123 ABC, and is generally referred to as the "reversed format". As with the introduction of the forward three-letter format, local authorities switched to the reversed one when they needed to. This meant that simultaneously three formats were in use; some authorities were still using the two-letter format, some using the three-letter one and some the reversed one.

Staffordshire was the first authority to issue a reversed format mark, 1000 E issued in April 1953. Readers will probably be interested to know that this mark survives as a personal plate. Staffordshire was the first authority to use the three-letter format and it is not surprising that it was the first to use the reversed format too. It only had two codes which could be used in three-letter combinations, RE and RF, as E clearly could not, so the authority was under-provided with codes in comparison with its vehicle population. Readers will probably be wondering why the first issue was 1000 E and not 1 E. Lower numbers were used for trade plates. Although these were in a different format, Staffordshire, like most authorities, avoided potential duplication in their reversed one- or two-letter issues where the same code had been used for trade plates to prevent possible confusion. These cautious bureaucrats would not have realised the "pool" of unissued numbers they had created would one day provide a "bonanza" for DVLA when it started auctioning desirable unissued marks. The second authority to start issuing reversed registrations was Middlesex which started with 1000 H in June 1953.

This was Liverpool's first reversed mark. It was issued in May 1958. The car is an Aston Martin DB5 and as these were manufactured from 1963 to 1965, this would not have been the first vehicle to bear this mark. The number is now on a Peugeot 5008. Europlate

When reversed registrations were introduced the British Cycles and Motorcycles Manufacturers and Traders Union wrote to the Ministry of Transport saying that plates with four figures in a row caused difficulties fitting plates to motorcycles. Then the Society of Motor and Manufacturers and Traders wrote saying that four figures in a row also caused problems for their members. On some cars and more specialist vehicles plate apertures were not wide enough to fit two-line plates with four digits across and on others the number plate light would not adequately illuminate a wider plate. These comments might seem surprising as quite a number of smaller Scottish authorities were still issuing plates comprising two letters followed by four numerals. Nevertheless, the Ministry considered this issue and decided to stop issuing reversed-format plates with four numbers until 1 January 1957 so manufacturers had time to redesign their products. Staffordshire halted reversed E at 2500 E and started issuing reversed ARE thereafter. The reversed E series was not recommenced until June 1958 when 2501 E was issued. When Middlesex reached 9999 H reversed AHX followed – they avoided using a two-letter code.

DL indicates this coach was registered on the Isle of Wight and it seems to be about to depart on a tour of the island. The Isle of Wight started reversed issues in November 1962 and 818 ADL was registered in April 1963. The coach is a Bedford SB5 with a Duple Vega C41F body. In December 1974 it was sold to Porters of Dummer in Hampshire, but what happened to it thereafter is not known. Peter Relf

Although four-figure codes could be used after January 1957, authorities were encouraged to, as far as practicable, avoid issuing reversed marks with four numerals to motorcycles. This frequently entailed using special sequences for motorcycles. When using their one- or two-letter codes without a third prefix letter, they might reserve numbers below

Short numbers are attractive as personal plates, but 5 COJ remains on its original Lancia Aurelia.5 COJ was issued by Birmingham in November 1957. Alistair Hacking.

1000 for motorcycles and numbers above 1000 for other vehicles. Alternatively, they might use three-letter codes for motorcycles and four-numeral combinations with one or two letters for other vehicles. Practice varied and sometimes motorcycles did get marks with four numerals. Some authorities started their reversed combinations with their one- or two-letter codes; others with their three-letter ones. Practice also varied regarding whether three-wheelers were treated as cars or motorcycles and some even differentiated between reversible three-wheelers and non-reversible ones.

Warrington (with code ED) is an authority which well illustrates practice in respect of motorcycle segregation. It decided to issue reversed ED rather than reversed three-

letter combinations when it commenced issuing reversed marks. To avoid possible confusion with trade plates, it held back 1 to 100 ED. It therefore started a block for motorcycles at 101 ED with a block for cars, etc starting at 1000 ED. When motorcycles had reached 999 ED, 1 to 999 AED followed for them. When 999 AED was reached in April 1964, possibly because they anticipated that year letters would soon be introduced,

West Sussex issued this number to this AC Greyhound on 13 February 1961. Alistair Hacking

rather than start reversed BED, motorcycles were integrated into the main series and given **** ED numbers.

If one discounts variations resulting from the desire to avoid numbers over 1000 on motorcycles, local authorities generally issued their marks in alphabetical and numerical sequence as with three-letter forward issues. As motor vehicles were becoming more popular, there was a significant increase in the number of firms and organisations running large vehicle fleets. It therefore became more common for whole series or at least large blocks to be reserved for these, thus affecting the normal issuing sequence. Coventry adopted the practice of having separate series for cars, commercials, motorcycles and Home Delivery Exports, so developed quite a complicated order of issue. Birmingham continued its practice of having separate series for commercials and Home Delivery Exports, so also had a somewhat complex sequence. London had special series for the Post Office and government departments, so its sequence was not always regular. Middlesex became slightly

less irregular than it had been with its forward three-letter issues, but still was far from consistent. For no obvious reason unusually Blackpool's reversed issues progressed from AFR to JFR with no marks from its other code, FV, being used at all.

The use of reversed combinations raised another source of possible confusion, in addition to that between ordinary issues and trade plates. Numbers like 1230 AB and 123 OAB could easily be mixed up. To prevent this the Ministry of Transport instructed authorities not to issue reversed three-letter combinations beginning with O. Unfortunately eight authorities overlooked this instruction; Bristol, Chester, Cornwall, Derbyshire,

Local authorities were not supposed to issue three-letter reversed marks beginning with "O", but West Sussex was an authority that did this in error as this photo of 348 OBP on a Morris Minor demonstrates.

Lancashire, Somerset, Surrey and West Sussex. All but Bristol, Chester and Cornwall realised the error of their ways and ceased issuing their "Os" part way through. Bristol, Cornwall and Somerset did not in

the end issue reversed two-letter combinations, so there was not a problem in these areas. Chester avoided the problem by not issuing any ***0 FM marks, but Derbyshire, Lancashire, Surrey and West Sussex did have "duplications". Lancashire obviously felt so contrite about their mistake that, although they were reached in the sequence that they omitted their Oxx combinations when

OO and WC were allocated to Essex in June 1961 as otherwise the authority would have run out of marks and OO was commenced in September 1961. The car is an Austin A55 Cambridge Farina. Europlate

they were due to be issued with C-suffix! Some of the withheld reversed O** combinations have now been sold in the DVLA auctions.

Car ownership was rising quickly in this period and two authorities were running out of available codes. One was Staffordshire again: the other was Essex. Readers may recall from chapter 2 that in addition to MN which was held back because of possible confusion with Isle of Man issues three two-letter codes remained unissued; BF, OO and WC. The decision was made to allocate BF to Staffordshire and OO and WC to Essex. Rules were set about how they could be used – BF and WC could only be used in three-letter combinations and ABF, BBF and UBF and AWC and UWC were not authorised. Perhaps surprisingly, all xOO trios including LOO and POO were considered acceptable, though reversed OO and OOO were not issued. The allocation of BF, OO and WC ensured the reversed system continued for longer.

CHAPTER 5 – THE INTRODUCTION OF YEAR LETTERS

Middlesex was the first local authority to start issuing year letters. Middlesex issued AMP 595A to this Morris Mini-Minor in April 1963. Europlate

Using the BF, OO and WC codes prolonged the six-digit format for a while, but another new one was again soon needed. The introduction of the MoT test resulted in a desire for the police to be able to ascertain a vehicle's age readily and year letters were the way to achieve this. Other advantages cited in Ministry of Transport files in the National Archives are being able to date vehicles when doing traffic counts and identifying whether older vehicles are more likely to be involved in accidents when analysing accident records, though to me these seem to be very minor advantages. The allocation of BF to Staffordshire meant that it was not that authority which was the first one to start using year letters even though it had been the first to use three-letter forward combinations and then reversed combinations. Rather it was Middlesex which issued AHX 1A on 18 February 1963. The format of plates was now three letters followed by up to three numerals and a year letter.

This change resulted in an increase in the maximum number of digits on a plate from six to seven and to keep the size of plates the same, the dimensions of the characters was reduced. Previously the height of characters was 3½ inches, but now it was changed to 3⅛ inches (now expressed as 79 mm in legislation). Number plate manufacturers did not want to be faced with a situation where they had to start producing plates with a different size of character all at once. It was therefore agreed that the introduction of year letters would be phased in. Authorities switched to year letters over 1963/4 with the final tranche switching on 1 January 1965. One consequence of the smaller sized number plate characters was the requirement to read a number plate at 75 feet to obtain a driving licence was reduced to 67 feet (now expressed as 20.5 metres in legislation). In the last chapter we learnt that most authorities tried to avoid issuing marks with four numerals to motorcycles. A number plate with three numerals and a year letter raised the same problems as a four-numeral plate. A lot of authorities reserved some or all numbers below 100 (or sometimes 199) with year letters for use on motorcycles.

Comparatively few A-suffix marks were issued in 1963 and if one seen today is more likely to be a re-registration issued more recently or a mark sold in a DVLA auction. Only 14 authorities started issuing year letters in 1963 and there were special reasons for each of these doing so. Four authorities switched as they were running out of marks; Essex, Lancashire, Middlesex and Staffordshire. Aberdeenshire, Bolton, Huddersfield, Northumberland, Oxfordshire, Plymouth, Salford and Stockport switched to avoid having to start reversed combinations. Motherwell and Wishaw commenced year letters as it was exhausting "forward" FGM and was not authorised to issue GGM.

Nottinghamshire was an authority that generally used numbers below 100 for motorcycles. This number was issued in May 1968. Note that the mark is displayed on three lines which is legal in this instance, though it would not be legal with a current-system plate.

The final authority to commence issuing year letters in 1963, Kirkcaldy, requires special mention. The last new registration authority to be created had been

![AXA 615A]

Doncaster which became a county borough in 1927. In the mid-1960s several new registration authorities were set up. Two Scottish burghs reached the 50,000 population limit in the 1961 census which qualified them to become registration authorities, Kirkcaldy and Coatbridge. With the commencement of year letters, London stopped using its X* codes and these were taken from it. XA and XB were given to Kirkcaldy and Coatbridge respectively; Kirkcaldy starting issuing A-registrations in 1963 and Coatbridge in 1964 (with B-suffix, of course). The other new registration authorities created were new English county boroughs; Solihull (XC) and Luton (XD and XE) in 1964 and Torbay (XF) in 1968.

As its population exceeded 50,000 in the 1961 census Kirkcaldy became a registration authority in April 1964. It took the code XA from London and issued AXA-A from April to October 1963. Europlate.

Another big change occurred in English local government around this time when the Greater London Council was set up on 1 April 1965. London absorbed Middlesex (which had many codes), Croydon (BY, OY, RK and VB), East Ham (HM and HV) and West Ham (AN and JD). The way the authority "absorbed" the issues from the non-London authorities was slightly complicated and it took a while for them to be fully integrated with London's issues. Five area offices were set up to issue registrations and each had separate series, though this was not administered on the basis of particular offices always using the same code letters.

Whilst considering local authority mergers, it should be noted that on 1 April 1965 the Cambridgeshire (CE, ER and VE) and Isle of Ely (EB and JE)

Bute which had the code SJ was the slowest issuing registration authority in Britain. When it went onto year letters on 2 January 1964, it had only issued as far as SJ 2860. The photos show one of the last 1963 issues and the second 1964 one. Europlate.

County Councils were merged into one authority as were Huntingdon (EW) and the Soke of Peterborough (EG and FL). In both cases the two former councils' registration offices continued to function separately until 1 April 1966. On 1 April 1966 Warley County Borough was formed incorporating the former Smethwick County Borough (HA). On 1 April 1967 West Hartlepool County Borough (EF) merged with Hartlepool to form the County Borough of Hartlepool. On 1 April 1968 Middlesbrough (DC and XG) was absorbed into Teesside County Borough. In addition, four joint registration authorities were established during the period when local authorities issued year letters.

Authorities	Merger date
Ipswich (DX and PV) and East Suffolk (BJ and RT)	1 April 71
Oxford (FC, JO and WL) and Oxfordshire (BW and UD)	20 March 72
Cardiff (BO, KG and UH) and Glamorganshire (L, NY, TG and TX)	26 March 73
Berkshire (BL JB, MO, RX) and Reading (DP and RD)	30 April 73

Normally a local authority's first year letter issue would be A** 1Y where Y represents the letter for the year when issues started, i.e. A, B or C depending whether they started in 1963, 1964 or 1965. Two Scottish authorities "got it wrong". Greenock was issuing forward EVS when it was due to start issuing year letters on 1 April 1964. It continued the EVS series but with a B-suffix added. Similarly East Lothian were issuing forward HSS when it went onto year letters on 2 March 1964 and followed on with JSS-B.

Until 1983 vehicles registered second-hand such as imported ones were given current year letter marks. FB Vauxhall VX4/90s were made between 1961 and 1964, but this one has an F-registration indicating a 1967/8 issue. This is because it was originally owned by an RAF pilot in Cyprus. SYH 520F was issued by the Greater London Council in September 1967.

The pattern of issue for year letter issues was basically similar to that used for forward three-letter combinations. There was, however, one complication. Provision had to be made for re-registrations which at that time were just replacement marks following personal plate transfers (vehicles such as second-hand imports were registered with a current year letter mark at this time). If a personal number was transferred off, say, a 1965 car, the local authority had to give it a replacement C-suffix mark. Most authorities made provision for this by leaving a gap at the end of each year's issues for re-registrations, before starting the next year's issues. Gradually, the alphabet would be worked through until Y** was completed and issues reverted to A** and a second cycle was commenced.

Not all authorities adopted the practice of having breaks between each year's issues, however. Most registrations by this time were allocated to new vehicles by garages. The licensing authority would supply the garage with a block of numbers and when a vehicle was sold it would be given a number from the block. At the end of a registration year some garages would have unused numbers as they had been issued with more registrations than they had been able to sell vehicles. Most authorities would void such numbers, but those that adopted the alternative practice would ask the garage to change the suffix to the following year's. Thus, in contrast to

the authorities which had a clear break between one year's issues and the next, some would have an overlap where for a range of numbers two different suffixes could exist. In many cases, such authorities would use a special block for each year's re-registrations. Some, however, would reserve a block for all re-registrations and change the year letter of the next number to match the age of the vehicle, e.g. Northumberland used YTY from circa 300 upwards for this purpose and any suffix letter from A to N could be found in this range of numbers. Some authorities ended up with quite complex patterns of issue; the largest and most complicated in this respect being Hertfordshire. It should also be

Hertfordshire was the authority which had the most complex pattern of year suffix issues as this example shows. Whilst most SUR marks had a D-suffix, about 150 had an E-suffix and this is one of them. The Austin Mini Cooper in this snapshot, SUR 549E, has not survived. Jonathan Del Mar

noted that sometimes local authorities would meet requests for particular numbers and year letters, e.g. although all other AUR's in Hertfordshire's relevant cycle had K-suffix, AUR 10L was specially issued so a lady called Auriol could have her name on her number plate.

One authority got the idea of working through the alphabet in cycles for year letters wrong. This was Dundee. They started with ATS-B and at the end of 1964 it was part way through AYJ-B and continued that series with C-suffix. Then they followed it with ATS-C, followed by BTS-C and part of BYJ-C. The rest of BYJ was used up with D-suffix before they started ATS-D. The Ministry of Transport heard about this gaffe from a somewhat surprising source; HP Information Ltd picked up that very similar marks were being issued each year. It seems that Dundee had already picked up that they were "doing wrong" as when the Ministry contacted them they replied that ATS-D had been "erroneously commenced by one of the assistants and on discovery....immediately rectified". ATS-D had been suspended at ATS 40D and CTS-D was then commenced. From then on normal sequence was adopted.

Another authority which adopted an unusual sequence was Staffordshire. In 1960 they had had BF "thrust upon" them as they were running out of available marks. As explained in the previous chapter, this could only be used in three-letter combinations, however, and ABF, BBF and UBF were not authorised for issue. It seems that the BF combinations were not very popular with Staffordshire motorists, probably because it was not a longstanding local code and therefore recognised as being a Staffordshire code. When they commenced issuing year letters they started using just their RE and RF combinations. Thus, the sequence ran ARE-A, ARF-A, BRE-A, etc. It would appear that they had doubts whether they really ought to have been doing this and on 12 August 1964, after they had been issuing year letters for over a year, wrote to the Ministry of Transport for guidance on this explaining the BF series had not been used as they were unpopular with motorists. The Ministry advised that omitting BF combinations would result in too many similar marks being

issued too close together and they should use the BF series. Thus, when YRF-C was reached it was followed by CBF-C to YBF-D. Their second cycle of marks ran ARE-D to YRF-H followed by CBF-H to YBF-J. Their third cycle started with ARE-J, but that cycle was still on the REs and RFs when Staffordshire stopped being a registration authority in September 1974.

The "E" suffix letter was only used for seven months, January to July 1967. This Ford Cortina has its number plate displayed on a vinyl strip on the bonnet; a method of display that was fashionable at the time, but not always popular with the police. – Rod Lomax

The problem with using year letters was that many people wanted to take delivery of new cars on 1 January and this created a peak in demand just as garage and registration office staff wanted to take their Christmas holidays. To overcome this the E period was shortened, lasting from January to July 1967 and thereafter the changeover point remained 31 July/1 August for a long time to come.

On 20 December 1967 legislation came into force giving motorists the option of using reflective plates; the front ones having a white background with black characters and the rear ones black on yellow. Before doing this the Ministry of Transport had the Road Research Laboratory carry out an assessment of the durability of these plates, using a number of vehicles which regularly used the A4 near their premises at

·6330 KX·

In the 1960s the Road Research Laboratory carried out trails of reflective plates. This photo, taken in 1965, features a trial vehicle. 6330 KX was issued by Buckinghamshire in 1963. – Reg Wilson

34

Crowthorne. From 1 January 1973 these plates became compulsory for most types of new vehicle; the exceptions being motorcycles, lorries over 3 tons carrying reflective markings, buses used primarily or entirely on stage carriage services, invalid carriages, works trucks and agricultural machines.

In 1971 the isles of Scilly were given their own registration code. SCY 314M was issued in March 1974. – Reg Wilson

In 1971 the Isles of Scilly were given their own code and SCY was chosen for that purpose, so it was "taken" from Swansea and passed to Cornwall for use on the Scillies. Thus, SCY from J-suffix onwards is a Scillies issue, not a Swansea one. This change occurred at the suggestion of the then Prime Minister, Harold Wilson, who had a holiday cottage on the islands.

The system whereby vehicle owners were traced was by now somewhat inefficient. The police or whoever wanted the details would contact the authority that originally issued the registration but would then probably be referred on another authority who now held the records as the vehicle belonged to somebody living in that area. Sometimes they might do that only to find that the records had now been passed to another authority. An example of the problems caused was when three policemen were shot in Braybrook Street, Shepherds Bush in August 1966. The police had the number of the Standard Vanguard estate car involved, PGT 726, but by the time they were in a

Vehicles first registered in August or September 1974 which are numbers issued by local authorities rather than Local Vehicle Licensing Offices can be readily recognised as they have N-suffix and the first letter is in the range A to F or N to Y. This Ford Cortina, TOL 789N, is such an example. The number was actually issued by Birmingham on 2 September 1974. The car is an interesting one. Ford did not make any convertible Cortinas, but some specialist companies made such conversions. The Crayford Company, based in Crayford, Kent, carried out his conversion.

position to contact the Greater London Council (GT was a London code) to get the owner's details the office was closed and somebody had to be called out. As it happened, in that instance the car was registered to a London address, but it would have been more problematic if the records had been transferred elsewhere. Of course, the computer had by now been developed to provide a more efficient means of storing vehicle details. This, however, necessitated records to be held centrally which meant they needed to be administered by the Ministry of Transport. The Vehicle and Driving Licence Act 1969 enabled the Ministry to take over the local authorities' roles of registering vehicles, levying vehicle excise duty and licensing drivers and that came into effect on 1 April 1971. Thereafter local authorities carried out these functions as agents for the Ministry until these roles were fully transferred to the Driver and Vehicle Licensing Centre at Swansea.

Though the Driving and Vehicle Licensing Centre (DVLC) did not start registering new cars until 1 October 1974 in the end, it was initially anticipated that they would do this on 1 January 1974 and it was necessary to have a means to enable local authority and DVLC M-registrations to be readily identifiable. The Ministry of Transport decreed that in the M year all local authority issues should be in the second half of the alphabet, i.e. the first letter should be between N and Y. Authorities which were in the first half of the alphabet at the end of the L year had to jump to starting their registrations with N and any which finished their cycle whilst issuing M-suffix had to restart the cycle at N, i.e. when they issued the last of their Y**-M marks they should skip A**-M to M**-M combinations and start with N**-M ones.

The date for centralisation at DVLC was then put back to 1 April 1974 and then finally 1 October 1974. Perhaps inevitably some authorities breached the ruling about issuing marks in the second half of the alphabet. This was particularly the case with authorities which did not cancel unused marks at the end of the registration year, but changed the suffix letter to the next year's. When it was realised that DVLC would not be issuing M-suffix marks but starting in the N-year, the instruction to issue marks in the second half of the alphabet was modified. It was decided that DVLC N-issues should start with letters in the range G to M and in August and September 1974 when local authorities were still issuing numbers, they should keep their issues in the range A to F or N to Y. This meant that vehicles registered in August and September 1974 were instantly recognisable by looking at the first letter on their number plates. This ability proved quite useful once when a friend of mine who was dabbling in buying and selling used cars mistakenly believed one of his stock was a 1975 one and I was able to tell him it was a 1974 model. This is one of the few times in life when an interest in vehicle registrations has proved something more than totally, completely, utterly and absolutely useless!

Local government reorganisation took place in England and Wales on 1 April 1974, but the registration authority reorganisation took place six months later, on 1 October 1974. In practice it generally seems to have been "business as usual" for this six-month period in England and Wales – the existing offices continued to issue their old codes for the same areas as if nothing had happened. There is one known exception. Birkenhead (BG and CM) and Wallasey (HF) plus parts of the Wirral peninsula formerly in Cheshire were combined to form the Wirral Metropolitan Borough Council and the registration function was taken over by the new authority. When this occurred Birkenhead was issuing WCM-M and Wallasey PHF-M. These two series were completed, but thereafter only Birkenhead's codes were used.

Another local authority stopped issuing registrations prematurely, Ross and Cromarty. This closed on 13 July 1973 and for a while no more JS marks were issued. Residents in more remote areas tended to be very attached to their codes and this caused an outcry among locals and in March 1974 Inverness started issuing JS marks starting at SJS 500M. It is interesting to note that following the establishment of DVLC in October 1974, although JS was "moved" to Stornoway, many Ross and Cromarty cars were registered in Stornoway so they could receive JS numbers.

The establishment of DVLC sadly resulted in the destruction of many local authority vehicle registration records, particularly for the larger authorities. Nothing or very little survives from the following large authorities; Birmingham, Liverpool, London, Manchester (F to N year letter records only survive) and Middlesex. If you want to look at old local authority records, e.g. to trace the history of a classic car or personal number you own, a very helpful list of surviving records and where they can be inspected can be found on the Kithead Trust website, www.kitheadtrust.org.uk.

CHAPTER 6 – THE DRIVER AND VEHICLE LICENSING CENTRE

In September 1974 the Driver and Vehicle Licensing Centre at Swansea started issuing registrations for new vehicles to be delivered on or after 1 October 1974. It should be noted that in 1990 the structure of the DVLC was changed and it became a government agency and its name was changed to the Driver and Vehicle Licensing Agency (DVLA). When established, the DVLC worked through 81 regional Local Vehicle Licensing Offices.

DVLC did not stop issuing number ones as ordinary marks until the commencement of A-prefix in 1983. OAF 1R was issued by the Truro office in October 1976 to this rare Hino lorry. Some number ones from this era have been transferred onto other vehicles and retained as personal plates, but the lorry bearing OAF 1R appears to have been scrapped and the number has been lost. Bernard Minton

The title of LVLOs was changed to Vehicle Registration Offices (VROs) on 30 March 1987 as it was generally no longer possible to renew tax discs at them. Finally on 1 January 2001 they became known as Local Offices as by then a high proportion of new vehicles were being registered directly with DVLA at Swansea under the Automated First Registration and Licensing system (AFRL) which we will consider later.

Though now transferred onto a modern car, FAT 15T was an ordinary issue by Hull in March 1979. FAT 61T which nowadays would be considered to look like "FAT GIT" was also issued. That too has been put onto a modern car.

The establishment of the LVLOs meant that the two-letter codes had to be reassigned. Generally local authority codes were transferred to a nearby LVLO. For example, Warrington LVLO naturally took over Warrington County Borough's ED code, but also DJ from nearby St Helens, EK and JP from nearby Wigan and TB from Lancashire. Lancashire's other codes were distributed as follows; TC to Bristol, TD and TE to Bolton, TF to Reading and TJ to

Liverpool. Although codes generally "moved" a short distance, a few did "shoot across the country" like TC and TF. The principle that codes containing S were only issued in Scotland ceased to apply as GS and VS went from Perth and Greenock respectively to Luton and WS went from Edinburgh to Bristol. It was probably just a coincidence but the principle that all Scottish codes contained G, S or V was restored as YJ, the only code that "broke the rule" pre-1974, was transferred from Dundee to Brighton.

This Triumph Stag was registered UVD 252S at Luton in November 1977. Shortly afterwards Luton stopped issuing "VD" combinations, the last series being WVD-S.

As explained in the previous chapter, LVLO issues started at G** 1N. Interestingly, by coincidence Peterborough's first issue was GAV 1N and, as this spelt "GAVIN", there were several requests for this, so lots were drawn to see who should get it. LVLOs usually worked through their codes in alphabetical sequence, but there were exceptions, e.g. until T-prefix, Chelmsford used its codes "inherited" from Essex in alphabetical order, EV, HK, NO, OO, PU, TW, VW, VX and WC, then its codes "inherited" from Southend, HJ and JN and finally its code "inherited" from Hertfordshire, AR. Although local authorities had often kept numbers below 100 for motorcycles when they issued year letters, none of the LVLOs continued doing this. The practice for LVLOs was to issue one year's registrations, to leave a gap for re-registrations and to then start the following year's issues. There were no overlaps, though sometimes an insufficient gap was left and in due course re-registrations passed the point where the following year's first issues started.

Although DVLC was issuing registrations for new vehicles, local authorities still carried out many functions such as retaxing vehicles, dealing with changes of ownership and processing transfers for vehicles they had on their systems. Gradually older vehicles were transferred onto the DVLC computer and local authorities finally stopped handling registration and licensing matters in August 1978.

The "How Many Left" website indicates that 39 Morris Itals are still taxed and one would presume comparatively few of these would be estates. PFD 776W was issued in August 1980 by Dudley.

In 1975 the requirement for motorcycles to carry front plates was abolished. The reason for this was these plates, when placed on top of the mudguard which they frequently were, caused a danger to pedestrian.

In the same year the St Boswells office was relocated to Selkirk. In the late 1970s, Lord Rayner, the then Chief Executive of Marks and Spencer, reviewed various aspects of the civil service and one of his recommendations was the closure of a number of Local Vehicle Licensing Offices, 28 in all, in 1980/81; namely Aberystwyth, Ayr, Barnstaple, Barrow, Bolton, Boston, Cambridge, Canterbury, Dumfries, Durham, Grimsby, Hastings, Hereford, Keith, Kendal, Kirkwall, Lerwick, Newport, Oban, Plymouth, Salisbury, Selkirk, Stirling, Stornoway, Stranraer, Warrington, Wick and York.

According to the "How Many Left" website, only five Fiat Strada 65CLs remain in this country – TDP 826Y is one of them. This car was registered at Reading in November 1982.

Particularly in more remote areas where the local codes were more readily recognised, the possibility of losing those to which people were attached caused an outcry. The decision was therefore made that nearby offices would be able to continue to issue the closed offices' codes. Practice in this respect varied. Isle of Wight residents would expect any new car to be delivered with their DL code and, when the Newport office closed, Portsmouth, which took over the responsibility for issuing DLs, continued to issue them to island garages as before. Similar things happened with many of the closed Scottish offices. At the other end of the scale, very few or no local marks were issued after the offices at Barnstaple, Canterbury and Plymouth closed.

When T-suffix was issued **G 1T and **T 1T combinations were withheld, though some have now been sold in DVLA auctions.

I, O, Q, U and Z were not used as year suffixes. It is not surprising that I, O, Q and Z were not used, but slightly surprising that U was omitted. This was at the request of the police who were concerned that U and V could be confused, although the way registrations are issued in alphabetical cycles meant it would be unlikely that similar marks with U- and V-suffix would have been issued. It is perhaps interesting to note that the Isle of Man did issue plates in the MAN ***U format, though on the Isle of Man suffix and prefix letters were used serially rather than as year letters. Anyway, the "Y-year" ended on 31 August 1983 and a new format had, of course, to be adopted.

CHAPTER 7 – YEAR PREFIX ISSUES

Issuing A-prefix marks commenced on 1 August 1983. The BX code was allocated to the Haverfordwest LVLO. The Citroen company procured a significant block of A-RBX marks for Citroen BX demonstrators from 246 to 545 and this is one example. Bernard Minton.

In July 1980, the government initiated a consultation exercise on what should follow Y-suffix. Two basic formats were put forward for the Secretary of State for Transport to consider; the reverse of the previous system, i.e. A123 CDE, or ABC 84 DE or its reverse where "ABC" was a serial element, 84 the year and DE was the code for the issuing office. The conclusion was that reversing the format was the best option. It is interesting to note that when the system was again changed in 2001 which is considered in the next chapter the reverse of the second option, was adopted.

Each office's changeover from Y to A was carried out in a similar way to previous changeovers with a gap at the end of the Y-year's issues left for re-registrations and then the new series was started, except the format was now the other way round, of course, e.g. Reading's last Y issue was in WJB-Y and its As started with A-WRX leaving, rather generously, WJO, WJM, WMO and WRD available for Y re-registrations.

One surprise with the appearance of A-prefix marks was that numbers 1 to 20 were withheld and issues started at 21. Personal plates were now very popular and the intention was to sell these off, but this was not to occur for some years. The practice of starting normal issues at 21 continued for B- to H-prefix and, as we shall see shortly, from J-prefix more numbers were withheld for sale. Also, no A55 or A550-9 combinations were issued as they could be read as "ASS", though some have now been sold in DVLA auctions.

One change that occurred alongside the introduction of prefix registrations was in how vehicles registered second-hand such as used imported vehicles

When year prefixes were introduced, vehicles imported second-hand were given registrations appropriate to their age when registered. This is a 1985 Trabant 401 Kübelwagen. Though the B-year was 1984/5, this Bournemouth registration, B433 VJT, was not issued until June 1996 when the vehicle was imported.

and ex-military ones were dealt with. Until 31 July 1983 these vehicles would receive marks with the current year letter. As a consequence a trade had built up importing cars from places such as the Irish Republic and the Channel Islands to obtain the latest year letter (Occasionally surviving examples of vehicles with "wrong" year

This photograph was taken at Cadbury's World in Birmingham and shows a vehicle specially built to promote Cadbury's Crème Eggs. Q943 VOG was issued at Birmingham in October 1995. According to the DVLA record it is a "Bedford Specially Fitted Van."

letters can be seen at classic car shows, etc). From 1 August 1984 such vehicles received re-registration marks appropriate to their age – until then, the only marks issued as re-registrations were replacement marks following transfers. This change in practice raised the dilemma that it was not possible to date some vehicles, e.g. because they had been imported with inadequate paperwork or they had been rebuilt using parts from a number of vehicles. For these vehicles, Q-prefix marks were introduced. Each Vehicle Registration Office's Q-prefix series started at exactly the same point as its first A-prefix series, e.g. Portsmouth's first A mark was A21 NTR and its first Q mark was Q21 NTR, though as

comparatively few vehicles receive Q-prefix marks, Q-series proceed at a much slower rate than the A-series, of course.

Early in the G-year the DVLC started withholding 666 as it is referred to as the Number of the Beast (the Devil) in the Book of Revelation in the Bible and some motorists were not happy to be given it. Then later in the G-year further numbers were withheld; multiples of 10 and 11 up to 100, i.e. 20, 22, 30, 33, etc, multiples of 100 and 111, i.e. 200, 222, 300, 333, etc, and various car model-related numbers.

Early on in the G-year, 666 was withdrawn as it is the Number of the Beast in the Book of Revelation, so cars with "G666" marks are rare. This number was issued in 1989 by what was then called the London North West office then based in Ruislip. The owner of this car obviously was not superstitious and decided to keep the number when he sold his car. Presumably he has a brand loyalty to Fiats as it is now on a Fiat Ducato MPV.

By now personal plates were becoming increasingly popular and DVLA was planning to introduce its Sale of Marks scheme, so they did not want to be issuing potentially attractive plates "for free".

For the H-year, the "multiples" were withheld and a different range of car model numbers than had been held back in the previous year and also 57 The withholding of 57 requires special mention. At that time the Heinz Company was celebrating its centenary and was holding a competition with 100 specially made "Heinz Metro" cars as prizes. As the result of cooperation between the Heinz Company and the DVLA Sale of Marks team, the number plates of the cars were H57 followed by a letter trio of the winner's choice.

During the "H" year DVLC made some BMW model numbers available for sale and this is such an example. H318 JPT is on a BMW 318i. – Bernard Minton

On 1 October 1990 telephone sales of the H1 to 20s commenced (nowadays DVLA sells such marks online rather than by phone) with prices starting at £200. On that day £1,000,000 worth of marks were sold. At this point I should perhaps say that the withheld A to G-prefix 1 to 20s were subsequently made available on the following dates; A – 1 August 1991, B – 15 January 1996, C – 6 April 1999, G – 3 April 2000, D – 30 October 2000, E – 6 October 2004 and F – 8 October 2008. The apparent early release of the G marks came about as a result of pressure from amateur radio "hams" as many have their callsigns in the format G, followed by a number followed by three letters, so they were able to obtain their callsigns as number plates. Later in the H-year various BMW car and motorcycle numbers were made available for sale, namely 75, 80, 100, 316, 318, 320, 325, 518, 520, 525, 530, 535, 730, 735, 750 and 850. These were marketed though BMW dealers on an experimental basis and not advertised generally, but this experiment did not last very long.

In the J-year comparatively few numbers were withheld, the "multiples" again plus 72, 147, 280, 560 and 747. 72 is the par value of a typical championship golf course, 147 is the maximum break in snooker, 280 and 580 were Mercedes-Benz model numbers and 747 refers to the Boeing 747 plane (the "Jumbo Jet"). These same numbers were then withheld up to the end of the "P" year. The H1 to 20 marks were put on sale on 1 August 1990, i.e. part way through the H registration year. The J marks for sale were first available on 1 May 1991, i.e. before the J registration year started, so potential purchasers of J registrations could buy their numbers before 1 August when they might be taking delivery of their cars. Offering each period's marks for sale ahead of that period has been the practice ever since. The range of numbers available with J-prefix was extended – as well as 1 to 20 the "multiples", i.e. 22, 30, 33, etc and 100, 111, 200, etc, were also offered. Around this time DVLA started withholding the more attractive letter trios such as BMW, PAT or TOM.

During the M-year, M155 numbers were withheld, but they were subsequently offered for sale as they look like "MISS". "Miss RMA's" number plate with a bunny emblem is not technically legal as only a Euroband or the approved English, Scottish and Welsh symbols should be used on number plates.

Generally the same numbers were withheld and the same numbers offered for sale for the K to P year, though there were some exceptions. In the K-year DVLA intended to withhold all K155s, as it looks like "KISS", but a few were issued in error. K111s were not available for sale as they could be doctored to look like "Kill". In the M-year M155s were withheld as they look like "MISS" and in the P year the P155s were withheld for obvious reasons. DVLA has now put the K155s and the M155s on sale, but I understand there are no plans to sell the P155s!

Practice regarding withholding numbers changed significantly in the R-year. The same numbers were offered for sale, but various "car numbers" were held back together with 21 and 25, but these were not initially offered for sale. Many years later, on 1 April 2015, however, all R-suffix marks which had not previously been normal issues in the range 21 to 31 or with numbers 121, 123 or 321 (the significance of these numbers is explained in the next paragraph) were put on sale. This is because DVLA was running out of prefix marks to sell in its most popular series such as names like JON and SUE. Subsequently further previously unissued combinations in earlier year letters have been made available in a rolling process and at the time of writing they have worked backwards to N marks which were released on 28 March 2017, M on 3 April 2018 and L on 9 April 2019.

All S121 marks were supposed to be held back for sale, but a few examples were issued as ordinary marks in error, so they were withdrawn from sale. S121 UHK is an example that was issued as an ordinary mark – Chelmsford was the office to blame for this mistake!

S-prefix was only issued for seven months, from 1 August 1998 to 28 February 1999. Although the year letter changeover date had been moved from the year end to July/August in 1967, the summer peak in car sales was causing problems for the garage trade and registration offices, particularly as it was in the holiday period. Furthermore, there were "knock-on" effects of cars requiring annual services a year later and MoTs three years later. The decision was therefore made to change the prefix letter every six months in February/March and August/September from the beginning of T-prefix. For S the range of numbers for sale was extended. Instead of offering 1 to 20 for sale, 1 to 31 were made available, reflecting the maximum number of days in a month and meaning motorists could have a number plate matching their birth date. 121, 123 and 321 were also added to the "for sale" list. A mistake was made with 121, however, and some were issued as ordinary marks as well as a few being sold, so all were then withdrawn from sale (though a limited number are now available on the Sale of Marks website). 560, 911 and 944 were also held back with S-prefix but not offered for sale. The numbers reserved for sale remained the same for the remaining prefix letters. Perhaps surprisingly, no numbers were withdrawn during the T and V periods apart from those offered for sale. Having kept no extra numbers back for the T and V prefix periods, for W, X and Y, the "DVLA censor" seems to have gone mad. All numbers ending in zero were held back, except, for no apparent reason, 840, plus another 59 numbers!

After looking at the rather convoluted issue of numbers withheld and DVLA's inconsistent practices, we now need to backtrack. 1 August 1994 saw the inception of a major change to the registration system, one which was eventually to lead to the closure of what were then called the Vehicle Registration Offices (VROs). This was the system known as Automated First Registration and Licensing, normally referred to by the acronym AFRL. Under this system, instead of having register a new car through a VRO, garages could do it directly with DVLA using computer links. The garage held a stock of tax discs so in theory somebody could walk into a car showroom, say they wanted a particular car and drive it away a couple of hours later. This meant that each VRO had to have two "parallel" series, one for ordinary issues and one for AFRL issues, though the AFRL issues actually came direct from DVLA at Swansea rather than from the VRO. The first garages to go onto AFRL were two Ford garages in the Bristol area on an experimental basis and the first AFRL series was M-GAE, a series outside the range of Bristol's normal M issues. Ford subsequently dropped out of the AFRL system for a while, but later rejoined it, but over the next few years all major car manufacturers switched to AFRL followed by some manufacturers of commercial vehicles and motorcycles.

From R-prefix onwards the pattern of issue for registrations became much more complex. Although AFRL registrations were issued by DVLA at Swansea, they used codes appropriate to the location of the garage. Thus, as has been explained, VROs had to run two "parallel" series, one for AFRL issues and one for other issues. Up to R-prefix VROs worked through their codes in alphabetical order and through the alphabet in cycles, though the introduction of AFRL made the order of issue slightly more complicated. At the beginning of the R-year AFRL was extended to include a number of additional car makes. Partly as a result of this the pattern of issues then became considerably more complex, so complex that to most observers the order of issue might seem random. One element of this complex sequence was that for some AFRL issues codes were sometimes used in the pattern previously used in Northern Ireland, e.g. with a code AB the sequence would be AAB, BAB, CAB, etc. Also, at least one AFRL dealer and in some cases all AFRL dealers were tied to one VRO code.

The onset of AFRL with less work being done by the VROs resulted in the closure of further VROs; Dudley and Sidcup in 1993, Haverfordwest and Huddersfield in 1994, Coventry, Ilford, Leicester, Liverpool, Stoke and Taunton in 1996 and Gloucester, Guildford, London Central and Swindon in 1997.

At this point it perhaps would be useful to look at the London VROs in slightly more detail. When the DVLC was set up in 1974 there were five London Local Vehicle Licensing Offices as they were then referred to; London Central, London North East, London North West, London South East and London South West. These were located in Southwark, Stratford, Ealing, Sidcup and Wimbledon respectively. Until its closure in 1997 the London Central one was always in Southwark and always referred to as London Central. Circa 1975 the North West one moved to Ruislip and in 1992 it moved to Stanmore.

During the P-year BMW went on to the Automated First Registration and Licensing scheme (AFRL) and P21 JKB was Liverpool's first AFRL issue. Reg Wilson.

Circa 1982 the North East one moved from Stratford to Ilford. The South West office moved from Wimbledon to Croydon circa 1990. By this time the "compass point" offices were generally referred to in the motor trade by their locations and in 1991 DVLA officially changed their titles to reflect their locations in recognition of this, i.e. Ilford, Ruislip, Croydon and Sidcup. In 1992 when the Ruislip office moved to Stanmore, it obviously changed its name as a consequence. As stated above, the

South East/Sidcup office closed in 1993 and the North East/Ilford office closed in 1996. When the Central office was closed in 1997 the South East/Sidcup office was reopened and the South West/Croydon one moved back to Wimbledon. I apologise for having to explain all this "musical chairs", but it accounts for how the London offices are referred to in the pre-2001 code list at the end of the book and the current system code list in the next chapter – I have used the offices' official titles. "Musical chairs" was being played elsewhere in the country as in 1996 the Hull office moved to Beverley and thereafter took on the latter name. Similarly in 2000 the Middlesbrough office moved to Stockton and also changed its name.

CHAPTER 8 – THE CURRENT SYSTEM

Before the DVLA Local Offices were closed EX was a code issued by Chelmsford. This number was issued in September 2018.

As the prefix system was drawing towards its inevitable end at "Y", the government consulted on what format the new system should take. Up to now the system had evolved, but now it was to change completely with the new format bearing no relationship with the previous one. The format adopted comprised the "area identifier", two letters indicating where the mark was issued, followed by an "age identifier" of two numerals and finally what DVLA called "the random element" of three letters, though the "serial element"

"C" standing for "Cymru" indicates a Welsh number. CX63 OEV was issued by Bangor in November 2013. Note the bilingual text at the bottom of the plate.

might be considered a better description. When the format was first proposed, the order suggested was the opposite with the random element at the front, but after further consideration DVLA decided that putting the place of issue at the front would help people remember at least some of the plate in situations like hit and run accidents. Thus the format of plates became AB12 CDE.

We shall now consider the three elements of current system plates in turn starting with the area identifier. The first letter is a mnemonic indicating the region where the office issuing the registration is and the second the office (I am conveniently ignoring the fact that registrations are now issued from DVLA at Swansea following the closure of Local Offices but these issues continue to be on a geographical basis using the areas of the former Local Offices). Having said that, for one first letter, K, covering Luton and Northampton nobody could think of a mnemonic. Furthermore, some "regions" have just one issuing office. The code list for the current system is as follows:

A Anglia — AA-AN Peterborough

AO-AU Norwich

AV-AY Ipswich

B Birmingham — BA-BX Birmingham

C Cymru — CA-CO Cardiff

i.e. Wales — CP-CV Swansea

CW-CY Bangor

D Deeside — DA-DK Chester

DL-DY Shrewsbury

E Essex — EA-EY Chelmsford

F Forest and — FA-FP Nottingham

Fen — FR-FY Lincoln

G Garden of — GA-GN Maidstone

England — GP-GY Brighton

H Hampshire — HA-HJ Bournemouth

HP-HV & HX-HY Portsmouth

HW Isle of Wight

K — KA-KL Luton to 2008. Post-2008, KA-KH

Borehamwood and KJ-KL Northampton

KM-KY Northampton

L London — LA-LJ Wimbledon

LK-LT Stanmore to 2007 Borehamwood 2007 on

LU-LY Sidcup

Manchester — MA-MY Manchester

& Merseyside

N North — NA-NN Newcastle

NP-NY Stockton

O Oxford — OA-OY Oxford

P Preston — PA-PT Preston

PU-PY Kendal

R Reading — RA-RY Reading to 2007

Theale 2007 on

S Scotland — SA-SJ Glasgow

SK-SO Edinburgh

SP-ST Dundee

SV&SW Aberdeen

SX&SY Inverness

V SeVern — VA-VY Worcester

W West of — WA-WJ Exeter

England — WK&WL Truro

WM-WY Bristol

X EXport bought — XA-XF For vehicles

VAT-free for export to an EC country

Y Yorkshire — YB-YK Leeds

(51 only) — YL-YU Sheffield

YV-YY Beverley

Y Yorkshire — YA-YL Leeds

(02 onwards) — YM-YV Sheffield

YW-YY Beverley

Vehicles may be seen displaying the "missing" letters J*, T*, U* and XG to XY (I, Q and Z are not used in regional identifiers), but these will have been bought from DVLA and are not normal issues. Having said that, during the 07 period, for reasons which are explained later, T* codes were used for Scotland in addition to the S* codes. The second letters after T "paralleled" those used after S, i.e.. Glasgow had TA to TJ as well as SA to SJ with 07, etc. Some letter pairs are actually only available for purchase and are not issued normally. We will examine these shortly. FO, FU, MN and NF are never used; MN to avoid possible confusion with Manx registrations and NF as it stands for National Front, the others are omitted for fairly obvious reasons.

Whilst normally when you see a current system mark beginning with "T" it has been purchased from DVLA, during the 07 period Scottish Local Offices would have run out of marks because some series were withdrawn and some were held back for sale. Thus, they were allotted the T codes too. TF07 VLU was issued by the Glasgow Local Office in July 2007. Don MacFarlane.*

When the current system was being introduced there was pressure from the Isle of Wight to have its own code and the island was given HW, H for Hampshire and W for Wight. Although this is an Isle of Wight number, the plate comes from a Chingford garage which presumably sold it second-hand.

After a draft code list had been circulated for consultation purposes, some changes were made. The residents of the Isle of Wight, who had been very attached to their DL code under the previous system, complained that they did not have their own code and were given HW, "H" for Hampshire and "W" for Wight. Some rejigging of the West of England codes enabled Truro to have WK on the basis K stood for Kernow, the Celtic name for Cornwall. Furthermore, it was realised that many cars in the Liverpool area would receive Manchester registrations, so the mnemonic for M was changed from "Manchester" to "Manchester and Merseyside". After the end of the first (51) "period", the changes to the Yorkshire codes shown in the table were made. We will look at this further in due course and the other changes to codes referred to in the table will also be explained later.

Unlike with the pre-2001 format, codes are not normally issued in alphabetical order, but as far as possible codes more likely to be initials are kept back and the less common initials are used first. For example, Oxford's order of issue is OU, OY, OV, OE, OW, OX (though Oxford has many more codes, all those in the range OA to OY, they have yet to be used). There have been two changes to how codes have been used as a result of local reaction. After Merseyside football fans, perhaps not surprisingly, objected to having MU on their cars, that code was "relegated" to becoming a spare mark and when Preston residents started seeing PO02 and took exception the office decided only to use PO in the winter period.

Moving on to the age identifier, as with the prefix letters from S onwards, this changes every six months on 1 March and 1 September each year. The current system started on 1 September 2001 and the sequence has been 51, 02, 52, 03, etc. 01 has not been used, though I suspect that at some stage DVLA will start selling these. There are effectively two "seasons" under the system, a "summer" one and a "winter" one. The age identifier number for the "summer season" matches the calendar year, e.g. 02 was issued from 1 March 2002 to 31 August 2002, but it is harder to work out when a "winter season" vehicle might have been registered though you can, of course, turn to the list at the back of the book to find out.

The introduction of the current system saw the use of Z on the random element of the plate, the first ever use of Z on "mainland" as opposed to Irish plates. This number was issued by Wimbledon in June 2013.

Readers might anticipate explaining the three-letter random or serial element would be simple, but it is not. One would expect that some trios would be censored as they spell rude or offensive words and that is the case. Furthermore, some are reserved for sale (again something that will be looked at in more detail later). It does not stop there, however. In the same way as many numbers, in addition to those offered for sale, were held back from W-prefix onwards, many letter trios are withheld. For instance, in terms of alphabetical order the first trio used is AAE. The letters held back are generally those more likely to be people's initials. Sometimes an office may complete a full cycle in a period, i.e. use all its available letter combinations – this is more likely to happen during the summer period when more cars are sold, of course. If this happens, it then starts a "second cycle" using the previously unissued codes. To demonstrate this, a first cycle would progress AAE, AAF, AAJ, AAK, etc and the second cycle would progress AAB, AAC, AAD, AAG, AAH, etc (AAA is reserved for sale). One point to note about the letter trio is the use of Z – until 2001, Z had only appeared on Irish plates. I and Q are not used, however.

When the current system was introduced, a standard font for number plate characters was introduced under the provisions of the Road Vehicles (Display of Registration Marks) Regulations 2001. This was mandatory on vehicles registered after 1 September 2001 but could optionally be used on vehicles registered earlier. Pre-September 2001 vehicles have to have plates which are substantially in accordance with the standard font. It had become fashionable to have italics or other fancy characters on plates and it was proving difficult for automatic number plate reader cameras to decipher these, so the practice was made illegal (though as readers will be aware, this requirement is not always followed). The 2001 Regulations

Interestingly the letter "O" and the figure "0" are identical on the standard font as this plate, EO06 OVN, demonstrates. It was issued by Chelmsford in March 2006.

also prohibit motorcycles registered after 1 August 2001 having front registration plates.

By the time the current system had been introduced, it had become the practice for many motorists to display the Eurosymbol on their cars, though this was probably technically illegal. It certainly was on a pre-2001 style plate unless the plate had less than seven characters or had an I or a 1 as it was not otherwise possible to meet the legal spacing requirements and still have a Eurosymbol. The new standard font characters were slightly narrower than the previous ones, so the Eurosymbol could be accommodated. Furthermore, the Order specifically provided for its optional

display. It did not, however, provide for the display of the flags of the countries that comprise Britain, although their use was also becoming popular. The regulations were amended by the Road Vehicles (Display of Registration Marks) (Amendment) Regulations 2009 which allow the display of the equivalent of a Eurosymbol containing the Union

In 2009 the Union flag and the national flags of England, Scotland and Wales were allowed on plates as alternatives to the Eurosymbol. This plate has the Scottish Saltire. As Hossack is a Scottish surname, this plate will have been purchase from DVLA. Don MacFarlane.

flag, the Cross of Saint George, the Cross of St Andrew (the Saltire) or the Welsh Red Dragon flag. It should be noted that a vehicle displaying the Eurosymbol can be used in a European Union country without having to display a GB plate, but if one of these other symbols is used, a GB plate must be carried. Assuming Brexit goes ahead, the GB-plate exemption in the European Union will no longer apply.

Interestingly cars registered in Northern Ireland are not allowed to display these other symbols. There is no symbol for Northern Ireland as there is not one which would be acceptable to both the nationalist and loyalist communities.

As this plate is on an Aston Martin and the surrounding numbers are on Fords, this mark would almost certainly have been purchased in the month when any mark may be purchased.

The sale of prefix numbers provided a significant income stream for the government and it clearly wanted to receive money from the post-2001 system achieves this is quite ingenious. Before marks are passed to the Local Offices for issue, for one month only all marks are offered for sale except those which are censored and those considered particularly desirable which are reserved for sale at auction. After that month the following categories remain for sale on their website and consequently are held back from use as normal issues:

1. "His 'n' Her Pairs". These are marks with the same letter at the end of the area code and the random element, e.g. AB12 CDB. These are likely to be particularly attractive to married couples.

Although "His 'n' Her Pairs" are primarily aimed at married couples, one presumes this mark was bought by somebody with initials "CPP".

2. Reserved Letter Pairs. Certain pairs are reserved regularly, although there have been some added to or removed from the list over time. Those regularly offered are AH, AL, BY, CY (to 55), DJ (from 57), DR, ED, EH, GB (from 03), GO, HO, JO, MG (from 03), MO, MR, MS, MY, NO, OH, OK, ON, OO (from 03), OR, OS, RU, SU, TO, TT (from 03), UK, UM, UP, UR, VD, VW, WC, XK and XX (from 03). Although I used the term "regional identifiers" to describe the first two letters on a current system number plate at the beginning of this chapter, for these pairs, it is a misnomer as the letter pairs do not indicate where the

"UK" is a reserved pair in the current system and made available for sale. This is a Porsche Carrera GT, so UK55 GTP (GT Porsche) is an appropriate number for it. Brian Gates.

vehicle was registered. It is interesting to note that few of these pairs are selected from groups where the mnemonic area code is shared between three or four offices, e.g. L, S and Y, as these are the "pinch points" in the system where offices are more likely to run out of marks if there is high demand for vehicles in any period. On the other hand there are quite a where only one office uses the first letter, e.g. Oxford (O). I presume VD and WC are included, not because they are particularly desirable, but rather because they are considered unsuitable for general release, but there is considered no harm in making them available for purchase. MG requires special mention. Although the manufacture of MG cars ceased in 2005 and has subsequently only recommenced in relatively low volumes, MG remains reserved for sale. MG, however, is quite common as a set of initials and this probably accounts for its continued availability. In addition to these letter pairs which are regularly held back for sale, others are made available when they spell a name or word with the age identifier, e.g. RO was held back in the 53 period as it looks like ROSE and CA in the 11 period as it looks like CALL.

3. Reserved Letter Trios. These are similar to the reserved letter pairs. More or less any random element that spells a name, e.g. BOB or SUE, a word, e.g.

CAT or MUM or a car make, e.g. BMW or JAG is held back and offered for sale.

4. Others. Sometimes a row of characters within a mark can make it attractive. Some examples which have been held back for sale are CO57 A** (COSTA), **10 TUS, (LOTUS), HE11 EN* (HELEN), *S11 NGH (SINGH), *W11 OW* (WILLOW) and BR14 N** (BRIAN). Combinations such as this are not issued as normal marks but put on sale instead.

Armed with this information we can now consider the reorganisation that occurred with the Yorkshire codes at the end of the 51 period and what happened with the Scottish codes in the 06 and 07 periods in more detail. The intention when this system was introduced was presumably to make the YA and YO marks available for sale regularly, but they presumably did not sell very well. Thus, they could be "put back into the pot" for normal issues and this facilitated a reorganisation of the

This appropriate number for this vehicle has obviously been bought for it from DVLA. As "GET" is a word, marks containing it are reserved for sale.

Yorkshire codes shown in the table at the beginning of this chapter. Whilst considering Yorkshire, it should be noted that in the 06 period all *W06 combinations were withdrawn. This meant that Beverley would have had insufficient marks with just YX and YY available, so Beverley issued YU which normally would have been issued by Sheffield. For similar reasons, Aberdeen issued SU, a combination usually reserved for sale as a "Select". In the 07 period, SC07 (SCOT) and SO07 were held back for sale (The reservation of SO07 might seem surprising, but all xO07 marks were kept back for sale in the 07 period because of the James Bond

SU" is normally reserved for sale but in the 06 period it was used for normal purposes by Aberdeen as SW06 was withdrawn. Don MacFarlane.

connection). Furthermore, SH07 (SHOT) and SN07 (SNOT) were deemed not socially acceptable and banned, so the Scottish offices could have ended up "dangerously" short of 07 marks. To prevent the offices running out of combinations, the T*07 codes were given to them and, as explained above, each office had the same second letters after the "T" as they used after the "S".

Whilst normally when you see a current system mark beginning with "T" it has been purchased from DVLA, during the 07 period Scottish Local Offices would have run out of marks because some series were withdrawn and some were held back for sale. Thus, they were allotted the T* codes too. TF07 VLU was issued by the Glasgow Local Office in July 2007. Don MacFarlane.

The Stanmore Local Office relocated to Borehamwood in 2007 and changed its name accordingly. In the same year the Local Office in Reading was transferred to Theale and took on that name despite vehicles registered there now having the wrong mnemonic as "R" stands for "Reading" not "Theale". The Luton Local Office closed in 2008 and Borehamwood and Northampton took over its codes. The ex-Luton codes have sometimes been used when the Borehamwood and Northampton offices have used up their own codes in a period.

With a high proportion of vehicles being registered using Automatic First Registration and Licensing (AFRL) and the increasing use of computers for other purposes, DVLA decided to close its Local Offices and to centralise services at Swansea. Although the civil service unions opposed this, it went ahead. The function of issuing new marks passed to DVLA at Swansea on 22 July 2013. Though the Local Offices were kept open for a few months longer to continue other functions, they were finally closed in three tranches between October and December 2013. It was estimated the closures would save £28m annually. In 2019 a new computer system, Register a Vehicle (RaV) was introduced replacing AFRL.

CHAPTER 9 – IRISH NUMBERS

Codes containing "I" and "Z" were reserved for use in Ireland. RI 44 was issued by the County Borough of Dublin and, as the car is a 1902 Argyll, this number may have been issued before registrations were compulsory on 1 January 1904. The car survives and still bears this number and is owned by Alistair Hacking. Alistair Hacking.

Until partition in 1922, what became the Irish Free State and is now known as the Republic of Ireland or just Ireland was, of course, part of the United Kingdom and the British registration system was used there. After partition, the two systems remained related up to 1987 and for a long time vehicles exported to the United Kingdom from the Republic or vice versa kept their original numbers. It might seem surprising that the Republic did not adopt a new registration system soon after independence, but the infrastructure of the country had been badly damaged by the Civil War and no doubt the government felt it had higher priorities. It should be noted that when partition took place Ireland's codes which had not been used already were divided up for future use by giving those ending in 'Z' to the North and those beginning with 'Z' to the South. In considering Irish numbers we will start with the North.

Although Northern Ireland remained part of the United Kingdom its registrations have not followed the pattern followed in the rest of the country, authorities starting by using two-letter combinations followed by up to four numerals. The first authority to exhaust its two-letter forward combinations was Antrim. Its original code was IA and it subsequently received DZ, KZ and RZ. Unlike 'mainland'

OZ was issued by Belfast from June 1950 to January 1953. Europlate.

authorities, it did not issue three-letter marks when its forward two-letter combinations were exhausted. Instead RZ 9999 was followed by 1 IA in January 1958 and then the remainder of Antrim's reversed two-letter combinations in the same order as its forward combinations were used. It should be noted that, although reversed IZ started at 1 not all Northern Ireland's reversed two-letter combinations did. As happened on the 'mainland' some Northern Ireland reversed series, including Antrim's DZ and RZ, started at higher points to avoid possible confusion with trade plates. As well as being the first Northern Ireland authority to start

In Northern Ireland when their two-letter forward combinations had been issued authorities switched to two-letter reversed combinations rather than using forward three-letter combinations. Reversed XI was issued by Belfast from June 1959 to April 1960. Europlate.

reversed combinations, Antrim was the first to use three-letter ones. When 9999 RZ was reached in January 1966, AIA 1 followed. Unlike on the 'mainland' forward AIA did not stop at 999, but ran through to 9999. BIA 1 then appeared, in July 1967. This sequence has subsequently progressed AIA to YIA, ADZ to YDZ, etc. In contrast to the 'mainland', in Northern Ireland I is used as a first letter in three-letter combinations, but not Q or Z (though ZIA has subsequently been used for vehicles bought VAT-Free for export to a European Union country).

Although 'I' is not used on number plates in the rest of Britain, it is in Ireland and it is used as a first letter. IIA 4319 which is on this Volkswagen Beetle was issued in early 1975 by Ballymena Local Vehicle Licensing Office.

Other Northern Ireland authorities have followed Antrim's pattern including using their codes in order of allocation, not alphabetical order. Year letters have never been used in Northern Ireland. From November 1985 numbers 1 to 100 were held back and from April 1989 101 to 999 were added to the range of numbers withheld. Then in November 1996 Northern Ireland started withholding multiples of 1000 and 1111 together with certain other 'nice' numbers like 1234 and car engine sizes like 1100 and 1200. In 1990 the series QNI followed by four numerals was commenced for use on vehicles of indeterminate age, the equivalent of Q-prefix marks used in the

In Northern Ireland the QNI series is used for vehicles of indeterminate age, the equivalent of Q-prefix in Britain. This kitcar is obviously such a vehicle. – Roberto Clark.

rest of Britain. These numbers were issued centrally, not by individual local authorities.

In October 1974 an equivalent reorganisation to the 'mainland' establishment of DVLC took place. Local authorities were replaced by local vehicle licensing offices with a central Driver and Vehicle Licensing Northern Ireland (DVLNI) office at Coleraine. In 2007 DVLNI was merged with the Driver and Vehicle Testing Agency to form the Driver and Vehicle Agency. In July 2014 the Driver and Vehicle local offices in Northern Ireland together with the central office at Coleraine were closed and their functions were taken over by the DVLA at Swansea.

Northern Ireland has always had a registration transfer system as in the rest of the United Kingdom, except there was no facility for retention certificates. On 28 February 1996 DVLNI started holding auctions, the first one being held by Wilsons Auctions, Newtownabbey. The most expensive lot was BIL 1 at £19,000 with £370,000 being raised from the 350 lots sold. All subsequent Northern Ireland sales have been held by Wilsons, a large Northern Ireland auction company. They have

This Northern Ireland auction mark, BIG 99, is appropriately on an ice cream van. John Black.

not only sold marks by auction, but also by tender and 'off the peg' online sales at a set price. With the incorporation of Northern Ireland registrations into the DVLA database, since the beginning of January 2015 the sale of Northern Ireland marks has been integrated with the British auctions, so each sale includes both 'mainland' and Northern Ireland marks. Also, selected Northern Ireland marks are offered on a "buy it now" basis on the DVLA Sale of Marks website.

In 2005 Enniskillen which had just one code, IL "inherited" from Fermanagh, was allotted a second code IG to prevent it running out of marks. It is likely to exhaust that code soon and DVLA has announced that, rather than allot it the only unused code still available for use in Ireland Enniskillen will start issuing reversed three-letter marks.

Before looking at what happened south of the border after partition occurred it is appropriate to highlight something that happened just before partition. This book just deals with the British and Irish Republic registration systems, but if one studies worldwide systems, there are frequent examples of political issues affecting the issue of registrations. An example of this phenomenon occurred in Ireland, however. Prior to the partition of Ireland, local authorities in what was to become the Irish Free State (now the Irish Republic) were not cooperating with the British government whose rule they, of course, detested and that included failing to administer the vehicle registration process and to collect the associated taxes. This resulted in the Road Vehicles (Defaulting Councils) (Ireland) Order 1921 which passed these roles to the Royal Irish Constabulary who presumably could be relied upon to fulfil these duties. One quirk of this provision was that, when the Constabulary took over the role, in Wexford (MI) the police issued numbers down from MI 9999 to 9923.

Moving on to consider what is now the Irish Republic, as has been reported, the country continued to operate the British-based registration system until 1987. Independence did, however, result in one change affecting registrations – for obvious reasons King's County became known as Offaly and Queen's County became Laois, though apparently no legislation was passed to formalise these changes. The sequence of marks the Republic has used has been two-letter forward, three-letter forward, two-letter reversed and three-letter reversed. I and Z, but not Q have been used as initial letters in three-letter combinations, though ZZ* series were not authorised. ZZP to 407 was,

A selection of old number plates off Irish Republic vehicles showing a range of plate styles.

however, issued by Donegal in error. Interestingly, the next series, reversed IH, started at 408 IH as a consequence. The progress of three-letter combinations has been in the same pattern as Northern Ireland, e.g. Galway which had codes IM and ZM progressed AIM to ZIM, then AZM to YZM. Having said this, Dublin was the first authority to start using three-letter combinations and in its first two cycle, GHI, IHI, SHI, VHI and ZHI were omitted and in the second cycle GIK, SIK and VIK were omitted, suggesting a link to the original 1903 Local Government Board reservations of marks containing G, S and V for use in Scotland and I and Z for use in Ireland. The reversed two-letter codes were used in the order they were first issued. Unlike in the North, in the Republic all forward combinations were issued before reversed ones were used. Authorities issuing reversed numbers used their two-letter combinations first before going onto the three-letter ones.

Although Z was not used as a code in the original 1903 allocation, it was issued by Dublin County Council between 1927 and 1940. Z 7071 is on a 1936 Ford Model Y which was no doubt assembled in Ireland as Ford had a factory in Cork. Note the unusual shape of number plate. Though issued in the Republic, this number is now on the DVLA computer.

In the Republic two joint registration authorities were set up. In 1952 Dublin County Council and Dublin County Borough Council merged to form a joint registration authority and in 1974 Cork County and Cork County Borough Councils similarly formed a joint registration authority. In 1982 the Dublin authority was running out of available codes, so new codes were given to it, SI, ZG, ZS and ZV, ones which had not been used previously as they contained G, S and V, letters reserved for use in Scotland when codes were allocated in 1903. Dublin initially used these codes in forward three-letter format, i.e. ASI to ZSI, AZG to YZG, etc. Only when YZV was exhausted in January 1986 was forward SI commenced. This was followed by forward ZG and then forward ZS. Forward ZV on its own was not used by Dublin as at the end of 1986 the authority was still part way through forward ZS.

When reflective plates were made optional in 1969 the front ones were white with black characters, but the rear ones were red with black characters, a not particularly successful colour combination in terms of visibility at night. Maybe this colour was adopted to clearly differentiate Republic vehicles from United Kingdom ones.

From 1969 to 1986 Irish Republic reflective rear plates were red. 154 OZI was issued by Dublin in February 1980. John Weeks

Albeit with a non-standard font, this is a plate with the format introduced in the Republic in 1987. The more normal font is that of the "MAN UTD" plate below.

On 1 January 1987 a totally new format was introduced using black characters on a white background front and rear. This comprised the last two numbers of the year, followed by a one or two letter mnemonic indicating the issuing authority, e.g. D for Dublin and WX for Wexford, and then a serial number. Thus a plate reading 87-D-12345 would indicate this was the 12345th vehicle registered in Dublin in 1987. In 1991 the Eurosymbol was added to the left side of the plate together with the name of the issuing authority in Gaelic in small letters along the top. In 2013, as a result of concerns that car sales might be reduced by buyers boycotting the unlucky number 13 and the system was producing a peak of car sales in January, the year was split into two halves with the numbers 131 and 132 being used for the two halves of the year. This practice has continued in subsequent years. Vehicles registered second-hand, e.g.

This P4 Rover was the first 1955 vehicle to be registered in Dublin after the current registration system was introduced in Ireland in 1987, so received the mark 55 D 1.

imported used, are given the next number in the sequence. Pre-87 vehicles are either given marks in this format, e.g. 61-D-123 for a 1961 car, or one commencing with ZV followed by up to five numerals (explained below), whichever the owner chooses.

Before 1987, registrations were sometimes transferred, though this does not appear to have been a common practice. With the change in format in 1987, transfers were prohibited. Since 1992, it has been possible to pay to reserve a particular number, however. The mayoral cars for Cork, Dublin, Limerick and Waterford have the number one. JJ Kavanagh & Sons Ltd, an Urlingford-based coach company frequently obtain 1, 11 or 111 numbers for their vehicles. Other examples of vehicles with these reserved numbers which can be readily identified are cars with appropriate 'car numbers', e.g. 323 on BMWs and 911s on Porsches with corresponding numbers. These reserved marks cannot be transferred from one vehicle to another. The reason for not allowing transfers is that Ireland does not want to have number plate dealers such as exist in Britain.

For many years, if a vehicle was transferred from the United Kingdom to the Republic or vice versa, it retained its registration number as the two systems were compatible. This practice ceased for vehicles brought into the United Kingdom from 1982 and for vehicles brought into the Republic from 1969. In the chapter on transfer procedures, it is stated that the transfer of Republic registrations was not permitted in the United Kingdom. In fact some such transfers took place in error, as Republic registrations looked similar to Northern Ireland ones. Therefore, from 14 December 1987 DVLA decided that all Republic marks on the DVLA

VIP 1 belongs to Russian billionaire Roman Abramovich and is an example of an Irish Republic mark now on the British system. David Nicholls.

computer, then estimated to be between 1,000 and 2,000 in number, would be transferrable to resolve the anomaly. The most famous Republic number on the British system is VIP 1. This was originally on the Popemobile used for John Paul II's visit to Ireland in 1979 and was bought by Russian billionaire and owner of Chelsea Football Club, Roman Abramovich, for £285,000 in 2006.

ZV is used for older vehicles imported into the Republic and this Ford AA breakdown lorry is an example of an early issue from this series.

Finally, mention needs to be made of two special codes used in the Republic, ZV and ZZ. Three-letter ZV combinations were issued by the joint Dublin County and County Borough motor taxation authority, but from 1992 ZV on its own has been used for imported or other vehicles over 30 years old. Although normal Irish two-letter marks were followed by up to four numerals, ZV plates with five numerals have been issued. ZZ has used for vehicles temporarily imported

into Ireland in a similar way to the United Kingdom's "Q" marks described in chapter 10 on Import and Export. These marks were issued by Dublin, the Royal Irish Automobile Club, the Automobile Association and authorities adjoining the border with Northern Ireland. ZV has only been issued in forward format, i.e. with ZV followed by numerals, but ZZ has been issued in both forward and reversed format. Forward ZZ, 1 to 9999 were issued from April 1925 to March 1983 and reversed issues started in March 1983 and are continuing. Reversed ZZ now uses five-digit numbers, i.e. numbers over 10000.

Both forward and reversed ZZ has been used for vehicles temporarily imported into Ireland. Europlate.

CHAPTER 10 – IMPORT AND EXPORT

This chapter deals with vehicles temporarily brought into the country or bought in this country with an intention to export it soon after purchase.

The International Convention on Motor Traffic signed in Paris in 1909 provided for the international circulation of motor vehicles. This issue is dealt with in more detail in chapter 19, but basically this permitted vehicles registered in one country to be driven in another without having to be registered in that country and having to display its number plates. This applied provided a plaque was displayed denoting the 'home' country; in the case of British vehicles this plaque was, of course, the familiar GB plate.

Provision, however, needed to be made for vehicles from countries which had not signed the 1909 Convention or the later ones or displayed number plates which did not use Roman letters. In 1921 the code QQ was allotted to the London County Council to be used for temporary registrations for such vehicles. These registrations were valid for a year, although road tax was due if they stayed in this country for more than four months. Though this code was officially allotted to the London County Council, it initially only issued QQ 1 to 999 and the numbers 1000 above were issued by the Automobile Association (AA) and Royal Automobile Club (RAC) acting as agents for the County Council. Most subsequent issues in these Q series have been issued by these two associations on behalf of the London County Council, subsequently the Greater London Council, then the London Central Office and finally the Wimbledon Office.

In 1930 QA and QC were allotted to the AA and RAC for these temporary imports. QS was allotted to the Royal Scottish Automobile Club, but it appears never to have been used and was subsequently issued by the RAC. Other Q* marks up to QS apart from QR, which we is dealt with in the next paragraph, were subsequently issued in whole series by the AA and RAC.

QC was issued by the RAC from 1931 onwards. The car is a 1953 Cadillac. Europlate.

QQ 2043 is an unusual example of a British registration that has been issued twice. It would have originally been issued by the AA or RAC in the 1930s and again by the London County Council in the 1960s to this Peugeot 404. Vic Brumby.

When London County Council completed their QQ 1 to 999 block in the mid-1960s something very unusual occurred. They continued on into the 1000s and up to 9999, although these numbers had been issued previously by the AA and RAC. It is extremely unusual for British registrations to be reissued, but this is one of the few instances when it has happened. In this case there was no danger of two vehicles being on the road with the same number as the numbers issued by the AA and

RAC would have been long defunct. When QQ 9999 was reached in 1979 London issues used QR.

The circumstances in which these Q temporary import plates could be used has evolved to being issued to vehicles temporarily imported which are:

- unregistered,
- with an overseas registration which has expired before entry into the UK or after entry if plates are to be returned
- when plates expire on leaving the country of issue, e.g. French trade plates.
- if the plate is not in Roman characters e.g. Arabic, Chinese etc.
- where it would be unwise to travel in the UK with plates from that country. The main category here was British Forces Germany troops visiting Northern Ireland or the Republic. This, however, ended up being self-defeating as it became known that BFG troops had Q-plates and ordinary tourists with Q-plates started to experience problems.

The motoring organisations issued these plates through their offices in the ports of entry. The numbers in these series were not issued consecutively, especially the AA ones. This was because plates were made up beforehand so they could be fitted when the vehicle arrived. They were made up in sets of two square, two oblong and square and oblong according to the shape of the vehicle's plate apertures, together with plates for motorcycles. There were also blocks for vehicles with unusual plate apertures whose plates had to be specially made. One would have expected the main category of vehicle to receive Q-plates to be French mopeds and small motorcycles which until 2004 did not have to be registered, but in fact few came into the country. This was because riders needed to have insurance and be able to meet the appropriate age qualification to ride a motorcycle or moped in Britain.

434 QC

434 QC was issued by the Automobile Association. The 'C' at the end would indicate it was issued in 1985/6. John Weeks.

used in forward format therefore. Making the second letter match the current year letter remained the practice when the format of British ordinary plates was reversed on 1 August 1983, i.e. reversed QA indicated a 1983/4 import, etc. The AA and RAC were each issued blocks within each year's issues and in addition a block was kept for the London Central office to issue. Around this time RAF Mildenhall in

From August 1981 practice changed and the letter after the 'Q' became the same as the year letter, i.e. QX coincided with the X-suffix registration year, etc. QV and QW were not

This is the format currently used for temporarily imported vehicles. The "10" indicates it was imported from March to August 2010 and the "456" is a serial number. - Jonathan Del Mar.

Suffolk also started being allotted blocks of these registrations for use on American servicemen's cars.

When the current registration format was introduced on 1 September 2001, temporary import plates changed the format 123 Q 09. In this format the trio of numerals are a serial number and the last two digits correspond with the age identifier – in this example the plate would have been issued between March and August 2009. The number trios started at 101 in September 2001 and have progressed serially subsequently with one period's numbers following on from the previous one, i.e. if 456 was the last number issued in one age identifier period, the next one would start with 457.

Having considered special plates for imported vehicles, we move on to special plates for those to be exported. Brief mention has been made in chapters 3 and 4 about the Home Delivery Export Scheme which was administered by Birmingham, Coventry and London. Under this scheme, a foreign national could take delivery of a car and buy it free of purchase tax on the basis they would shortly be exporting it. Though

Though it is not apparent as this photo is reproduced in black and white, the band round this plate is yellow as reversed EGX was issued by London from April 1963 to January 1964 as a Home Delivery Export Series. This Mark III Ford Zephyr obviously ended up being used as a Bahamian Government vehicle as the "135" number plate indicates. Vic Brumby.

Though again not apparent as this photo is reproduced in black and white, when reflective plates were introduced the band round Home Deliver Export Plates was changed from yellow to red. C311 BHX was issued to a Ford Capri on 8 August 1985. John Weeks.

the plates were in standard format, sometimes these authorities used special series or blocks for them. What more readily distinguished these plates was they had a thin yellow band surrounding them. This practice was introduced in 1965. With the introduction of reflective plates, in 1973 this was changed to a red band. The use of these bands was not a legal requirement, but rather encouraged by Her Majesty's Customs.

In January 1993 a new format of plate was introduced for 'means of transport' bought VAT-free in Britain for export to another European Union country. 'Means of transport' might seem a somewhat clumsy expression and one would think that 'road vehicle' or a similar expression might be preferable. There is, however, a provision in European legislation whereby one can buy any means of transport such as a ship, boat or plane as well as a motor vehicle VAT-free in one county for export to another with the VAT being payable in the second country. Part of the requirements of this provision is that there should be special plates for motor vehicles which have been

purchased under it. The format adopted in Britain was the appropriate year letter, three numerals and three letters; the last two of which would be XP, e.g. K123 AXP. The first letter of the trio indicated the month, with A for January, B for February up to M for December (I was not used, of course).

The 'L' and 'C' letters on this EU export plate, L69 CXP, tell us that the number was issued in October 1993. Reg Wilson.

With the change to the current system in September 2001, the format changed to one matching that for normal plates, but with the first two letters in the range XA to XF, e.g. XA51 ABC. The second letter indicates the month of issue. The first one in each age period is A, i.e. XA indicates either March or September, XB indicates April or October and so on to XF for February or August. The two numerals are the usual age identifier and the last three letters are serial, the sequence reverting to the beginning of the alphabet at the start of each month.

This mark was issued in June 2012 to a vehicle bought for VAT-free export to a European Union country. Alexander Kavka.

CHAPTER 11 – AGE-RELATED RE-REGISTRATIONS

Whilst this is probably an interesting topic for all registration and classic car enthusiasts, it is particularly important for somebody contemplating buying a classic vehicle. If a classic vehicle has lost its original number this affects its value and this should be factored in when deciding what to pay for it. Most personal numbers in circulation are marks originally born by classic vehicles and, if you are considering buying a vehicle which has lost its number in this way, it is worth less than an equivalent vehicle still bearing its original number. I perhaps should explain that technically all re-registrations are age-related as they would incorporate an age-identifier appropriate to the vehicle's age, but this term is generally used when referring to re-registrations given to pre-1963 vehicles. This chapter relates to the latter type.

The Austin A40 Cambridge was manufactured from 1954 to 1957, so you might be wondering why this was has a C-suffix registration suggesting it is a 1965 car. After 1977 when a number was transferred off a pre-1963 car it would normally be given an A- or B-suffix mark, but occasionally C- or D-suffix ones were used as this example from Birmingham shows. Bernard Minton.

When personal numbers started becoming popular in the early 1970s many numbers were being transferred off pre-1963 vehicles which were then given the next available suffixless mark as a replacement mark, e.g. Oxfordshire's last suffixless issue before it went onto year letters on 6 November 1963 was YUD 800 and YUD 801 upwards were used for re-registrations. It soon became obvious that a pre-1963 vehicle could become a "machine" for "producing" dateless registrations by transferring numbers from it repeatedly and many number plate dealers took advantage of this. In response many authorities stopped issuing low numbers and other "nice" numbers such as multiples of 100 and 111 as re-registrations.

Practice changed more significantly on 10 January 1977 when issuing suffixless numbers as replacement marks following a number plate transfer ceased. Instead a suffixed mark was issued, usually an A or B one, but sometimes a C or even D, depending on what suitable marks the issuing office had available. Exceptions were often made for veteran vehicles and also some newer imported vehicles which were still given suffixless marks. For this purpose the following series seem to have been used on a national basis:

At one time Bournemouth registrations were reissued when older vehicles were imported. EL 1758 on this 1915 Ford Model T is such an example.

EL – This was Bournemouth's first series which was issued from 1903 to 1924. Some EL marks were reissued for veteran and vintage vehicles; three-digit numbers being used for veteran vehicles, i.e. up to 1904, and four-digit ones for vintage ones, i.e. 1905-30.

WFX – Dorset's last normal issue was VTK 492, plus 500 issued early to meet a request for an attractive number. The County Council issued re-registrations to WFX 270 and WFX 271 onwards were used on a national basis for 1931 to 1955 vehicles. The series reached at least WFX 527.

Reversed DEL – Bournemouth's last normal issue was 666 CLJ. Re-registrations continued to 999 CLJ followed by 1 to 999 CRU and then 101 to 260 DEL. 301 DEL to at least 492 DEL were used for 1931 to 1955 vehicles.

DFP – Rutland's last normal issue was DFP 136 with some higher numbers used for re-registrations apparently in a somewhat random pattern. DFP 401 to 601 were then used for 1931 to ca 1955 vehicles.

This 1950 Vincent 500cc motorcycle displaying 423 DEL is an example of a reversed DEL re-registration mark. This one was issued in June 1981. Cliff Thoroughgood.

SL – Clackmannan's last normal issue was SL 9602 and re-registrations continued to SL 9699. SL 9701 upwards were used for vintage vehicles.

DS – Peebles issued normal marks up to DS 6396 and re-registrations went up to DS 6573. DS 6574 upwards were used for veteran and vintage vehicles.

As explained in chapter 7 until year prefix letters were introduced on 1 August 1983 vehicles registered second-hand such as imported ones or ex-military ones were given current year letters. From that date they were given marks with a year letter appropriate to the vehicle's age. Subsequently, on 1 December 1983 some new series for pre-63 re-registrations were started. The series used from this date are:

Veteran vehicles, i.e. up to 1904 – BS 8*** marks (Orkney had issued up to at least BS 7938). This series is still in use.

Pre-1930 – DS marks (continuing the existing series)

1931 to 1955 – Three-letter forward marks, starting with ASV, BSV, CSV, etc.

This 1924 Ford Model T was imported in 1992 when DS was in use for age-related re-registrations and it received DS 9972.

1956 to 1963 – A-suffix marks. For this purpose each LVLO created its own A-suffix series, frequently beginning with A, i.e. A**-A.

From 2 December 1991, 1956 to 1962 vehicles were given forward three-letter marks and owners of 1956 to 1962 vehicles which had been given A-suffix marks could have them re-registered with a suffixless mark on request. From then on such suffixless re-registrations were made non-transferrable, though sometimes errors are made in this respect and these marks do sometimes appear on modern vehicles.

Although suffixless marks issued after 2 December 1991 are supposed to be non-transferrable, sometimes they slip the net. This is an example on a car once owned by the author.

In November 2003, 1931 to 1962 vehicles started receiving reversed marks instead of forward ones, commencing with reversed UXA. Presumably it was eventually realised that such marks did not look very appropriate on pre-1953 vehicles and from July 2014, 1931 to 1952 cars started receiving forward marks beginning with YVL.

Although rules have been set out for what type of mark should be issued to what age of vehicle, it seems that sometimes mistakes are made and vehicles get marks in the wrong format, e.g. there is a regular participant with an A-suffix mark in the London to Brighton Run though the event is only for veteran cars. It should be noted that nowadays, as with local authority yearless re-registrations after year letters were introduced, "nice" numbers are omitted from these age-related series, such as multiples of 100 or 111, and for three-letter series the starting point is 101. Withheld numbers in these series have been sold through DVLA auctions.

The number plate of this 1942 Dodge ambulance may not be immediately obvious, but it is 201 BSV. A very few reversed ASVs and BSVs were issued as age-related re-registrations to 1931 to 1955 vehicles and this is an example.

It is thought that a list of series which have been used for these age-related re-registrations would be helpful. As mentioned above, one of these may indicate that a vehicle has lost its original number and this will affect its value. An inappropriate suffix letter could also indicate this, but it might also indicate a vehicle which has been registered second-hand, e.g. because it was imported, before 1 August 1983:

Pre-1905 – BS 8001 to 8999

1905 to 1930 vehicles – SL 9707 up, DS 6574 up, SV 4001 up, BS 9001 up, BF 4001 up. AS from 4148 up, NS from 5757 up, SJ from 2878 up and WC are available for future use.

1931 to 1955 vehicles, then 1931 to 1962, now 1953 to 1962 – ASV - YSV, a few reversed ASV and BSV were then issued, CSU – YSU, BSK - YSK, GVS – YVS, TYJ – YYJ, KFF – YFF, GFO - YFO (UFO omitted), PSY – YSY, ASJ – YSJ, ASL - YSL, AAS – YAS (BAS omitted as it is Gaelic for 'death'), UXG, reversed UXA – UXY, reversed XUA – XUY (XUO omitted), reversed YUA – YUY (YUO omitted), reversed UYE to UYY, reversed XVA to XVN, reversed XVP to XVS, reversed XVU, reversed XVV, reversed XVY, reversed YVA-YVS, reversed YVU, reversed YVY

BS 8*** marks are being used for veteran age-related re-registrations and BS 9001 upwards for 1906 to 1930 ones. Thus, BS 9001 on this 1926 Norton motorcycle was the first in the series.

1931 to 1952 vehicles – YVL, WXG, XBV, YWG , YXG, VXS, UXS, XVV, YXS, KXS, LXS

Practice has not always been consistent regarding the issue of replacement marks following transfers. Although this Fordson E494C van dates from 1950, when its original number was transferred off it in 1986 Luton gave it an A-suffix mark, BGS 592A, though it should have had a suffixless one.

Although perhaps slightly off-topic in this chapter, it is appropriate here to deal with what are referred to as "unclaimed marks". As suffixless marks were becoming quite valuable and some fraud was taking place in obtaining old numbers, DVLA set a deadline whereby any marks that had not been put onto its computer had to be entered onto it by 30 November 1983. Whilst this provision was publicised, inevitably many vehicles stored in lock-up garages, barns, etc did not get their marks claimed. DVLC initially insisted that any such vehicles which were put back on the road had to be re-registered. They then relented slightly in saying vehicles with such unclaimed marks could get their original numbers back if they were of significant historic interest. In 1990 a new scheme was introduced that, provided documentary evidence of the vehicle's number could be produced and an appropriate motor club for that type of vehicle supported the application, the number could be reissued on a non-transferrable basis.

CHAPTER 12 – PLATES FOR SPECIAL PEOPLE: MONARCHS, DIPLOMATS, MAYORS AND PRIME MINISTERS

Although originally the monarch did not have number plates on his cars, since 1936 only the monarch's official cars have had the benefit of this concession. This photo of a Daimler taken some time ago, of course, shows one of the official royal cars. Europlate.

I once saw a Rolls-Royce Phantom on the M1 with no number plates and knew instantly whose car it was. In Britain the Crown does not need to comply with legislation unless that legislation specifically says so. After the Motor Car Act was passed in 1903, the King did not have to have number plates on his cars. The "Dundee Courier" of 15 August 1922 tells a "Keystone Cops" story of the problems caused when five of the King's cars were brought to that city by boat to be driven on to Balmoral for a hunting party and the Dundee Police who did not know that King's cars did not require number plates pursued them. The cars in that instance did display the Royal Coat-of-Arms. In 1936 practice changed and from then on only the Monarch's official cars benefit from the concession not to need plates. The present Queen does have a number of personal plates, including A 7 on a 1900 Daimler Tonneau, the first royal car purchased by Edward VII, JGY 280, JGY 280K, JYV 1D, KUV 1, MKV 11 (on a Jaguar Mark VII), MYT 1, MYT 2, MYT 3 and PYN 1F. When she was Princess Elizabeth, she had HRH 1 on a Daimler given to her as a wedding present from the Royal Air Force, but that mark was surrendered on her accession to the throne.

Some other registrations associated with the Royal Family are A 100 and 1420 H belonging to the Princess Royal who was the Commander-in-Chief of the 14th/20th

King's Hussars, NXH 1 belonging to the Duke of Edinburgh and YR 11 belonging to the Duke of Kent. AMP 1P was specially issued out of sequence for the marriage of Princess Anne and Captain Mark Phillips. Princess Margaret used to have PM 6450, the 6450 reputedly indicating the date she met Group Captain Peter Townsend.

There are two special types of registration for diplomatic personnel. There also used to be a third type which were used for a short period but have now been discontinued which we will also examine.

Many embassies and high commissions have a 'personalised' registration for their Ambassador's or High Commissioner's official car. Some international organisations have such marks too, e.g. 1 MO for the International Maritime Organization. Also, for Australia and Canada, as well as the High Commissioner having such a mark, the Agent-Generals of each province or state generally have one. When Nigeria had federal status for a short time separate plates were also used for the Agent-Generals for the Eastern, Northern and Western Regions, 1 ERN, NN 1 and WRN 1.

Many embassies and high commissions have a special number for their ambassador's or high commissioner's car, but the Dutch Embassy has two such special numbers, NL 1 and NL 2. This photo clearly taken many years ago shows NL 2 on a Fiat 1100 complete with a "GB" plate and a "CD" one, standing for Corps Diplomatique. Europlate.

These plates normally comprise two or three letters which are a mnemonic for the country followed by or preceded by a number 1. Malaysia has 1 M, however. Jordan has HKJ 111, St Vincent 2 SVG and Thailand THA 11. A few countries have "year letters", e.g. BEL 12E (Belize), OMA 1N (Oman) and SPA 1N (Spain). Some countries have had such marks in the past but have abandoned them for security reasons, e.g. Israel (ISR 1) and the United States (USA 1).

The first mark to be issued under this scheme was New Zealand's NZ 1 in April 1949. A member of the New Zealand High Commission staff saw a car with an NZ number in Northern Ireland and approached the province's then Premier,

1 EE is the number of the official car of the Ethiopian Ambassador. Jonathan Del Mar

This is the official car of the High Commissioner for Papua New Guinea, NG is one of Norfolk's codes. Norfolk did not issue any reversed yearless marks, so this clearly is a special issue.

Sir Basil Brooke, to enquire if one could be issued to the Commission. Although NZ 1 had already been issued, the owner of it agreed to surrender the mark, so it could be used by the High Commission. The next one was Pakistan's PAK 1, also in 1949. The then High Commissioner, Habib Rahimtoola, requested it for his then newly acquired American car. Bradford which had the AK code had not reached PAK and a special Order, the Road Vehicles (Registration and Licensing) Regulations 1949 had to be passed to permit this, though subsequent issues have not been so authorised. For obvious reasons PAK 1 has now been replaced by 1 PAK. A few of these special marks were issued in the 1950s, but they became much more common in the 1960s and nowadays a high proportion of missions have them. Generally these special diplomatic plates are ones which could have been (and in some cases have previously been) issued as normal registrations, but there are several which would not as they commence with I, Q or Z, namely IND 1 (India), IRL 1 (Ireland – no longer in use, but the vehicle that bore the number was exported to the Irish Republic and is on the Irish registry still with this number), ISR 1 (Israel – no longer in use), ITA 1 (Italy), QLD 1 (Queensland, Australia), QTR 1 (Qatar), QUE (Quebec Province, Canada), ZAI 1 and 1 ZAI (Zaire – no longer in use), ZAM 1 (Zambia) and ZIM 1 (Zimbabwe). Examination of files in the National Archives reveals that when the first of these marks was requested, IND 1 in 1959, there was some "soul searching" by civil servants before the mark was issued. Recently REC 001 has been specially issued for the Cambodian ambassador. Marks with lead zeros are not normally issued, though as explained in Chapter 1 some were issued before 1921 for heavy motor cars. It is presumed "REC" stands for "Royal Embassy of Cambodia".

The second type of diplomatic regist rations are in the form 123 D 456 or 123 X 456. D is used for the official vehicles and X for consular and other accredited non-diplomatic personnel. These plates were introduced in January

Normally diplomatic numbers are on ordinary cars, but 135 D 341 is on a minibus. The author has even seen a double-decker bus with diplomatic plates! The 135 denotes the Chinese embassy.

1979. For diplomatic missions, the first three numerals normally indicate the relevant country. Originally 101 to 282 were allocated in alphabetical order going from Afghanistan to Zambia, but numbers now run to 330 as additional missions have been established. There are some higher numbers used for security purposes. Numbers above 900,

An "X" indicates a vehicle belonging to consular and other accredited non-diplomatic personnel. Numbers above 900 indicate vehicles attached to international organisations – in this case 908 is the International Cocoa Organization. Alexander Kavka.

however, are used for international organisations such as the Council of Europe and the World Health Organization. The last three numerals on the plate are serial. From around 1990 the actual plates have been officially issued as they incorporated security features; DVLA written repeatedly in a faint wavy line across the plate and the numerals, but not the letter, being in a narrower style, but for the last few years they have reverted to normal style but with no supplier's name or other markings on them. Diplomatic and trade plates are the only British types of plate officially supplied – in many other countries all plates are supplied by the authorities.

This is one of the very few RXS marks issued to diplomats' third vehicles. This number was issued on 24 May 1984, John Weeks.

The discontinued format of diplomatic plates were used from March 1984 to 1987 for the third or subsequent vehicles of diplomats. These comprised the letters RXS, a serial number starting at 21 and the year suffix or prefix appropriate to the vehicle's age, e.g. RXS 21X and A21 RXS. These plates were in normal format and, unlike the 'D' and 'X' plates, remained on the car when it was sold. Very few of these plates were issued – it has been estimated around 30.

We now move on to mayors or lord mayors. Actually we are considering more than mayors here as some of the plates are for the use of chairmen (or chairwomen, of course) of county councils and provosts or lord provosts of Scottish burghs. Many local authorities have of have had a special plate on their mayoral, etc car. I have used the term 'have had' as in recent years, faced by straightened financial circumstances, quite a few authorities have sold their plates off to raise much-needed money. The most notable such disposal was by

The original vehicle bearing Warrington's first registration was scrapped, so when £5 reissues were introduced in 1955 Warrington could use ED 1 for its mayoral car.

Essex County Council in 2008. The authority actually had special plates for the cars of its chairman and vice-chairman, F 1 and 1 F. F 1 was, of course, the first registration issued by Essex. 1 F was not Essex's first reversed issue – that was 1 AEV in June 1954 – but the two plates made a "matching" pair. 1 F was sold first for £144,500, but when F 1 sold it was for then a record price for a British plate, £440,000 in 2008. The purchaser was Afzal Kahn, who is a property developer and runs a company carrying out high quality car customisation. He is reputed to have subsequently turned down an offer of £6 million for the plate and it is now currently for sale, at a price reported as being £10 million. Incidentally, to prevent the Essex chairman having to ride in a car with an ordinary plate, before selling F 1 and 1 F, Essex had acquired ECC 1 for use on the chairman's car, though "CC" indicates it was a Caernarvonshire issue.

Most mayoral, etc cars have a registration issued by the relevant authority when they performed the function of registration authorities, frequently with two or three letters followed by (or sometimes preceded by) a number 1, e.g. DH 1 (Walsall), ED 1

HJ 1 was the first number issued by Southend when it became a separate county borough in April 1914 and that number is now on its mayoral car.

(Warrington), TS 1 (Dundee), CCH 1 (Derby), OBB 1 (Newcastle upon Tyne) and 1 VHX (Enfield). Some of these marks were resurrected as £5 reissues in the 1950s or 1960s. Barnsley's mayor travels in a car grandly bearing THE 1, HE having been Barnsley's registration code up to 1974. Some authorities' mayoral numbers are mnemonics for the authority, e.g. LBB 1L (London Borough of Bromley) and Solihull's SOL 1. Coventry's mayor is carried in 1 COV, a number issued by near-neighbour and rival city Birmingham! Leicester has two official cars, nicely registered ABC 1 and 1 ABC respectively, BC being one of the city's registration codes. Hastings used to have a special registration for the mayor's car and one for the deputy mayor's. The mayor had DY 1, DY being Hastings's code and the deputy mayor had an ingenious DY 1066. DY 1 has now been sold off, however, and the mayor now travels in DY 1066. One mayoral car number with an unusual explanation is 1 BBB. This was on Bridlington's mayoral car, its significance being three letter Bs appeared on the city's shield, but Bridlington is now covered by the East Riding of Yorkshire Council who have retained the number. In Chapter 5 on the introduction of year letters we learnt that XA and XB were allotted to Kirkcaldy and Coatbridge in the early 1960s. The first registrations to be issued by these authorities, AXA 1A, AXB 1B and AXC 1B were bagged for the authorities' provostal cars.

Other mayoral numbers are interesting from a registration perspective. Croydon used 1 BY and 1 VB specially for mayoral cars, the first numbers in these two reversed series, of course. Although BY was fully issued from 1 to 9999, other issues of VBs started at 501 to avoid possible confusion with trade plates as explained in chapter 4. Dudley's first reversed registration was 1 FD, issued in March 1959, whereas normal reversed registrations did not start till June 1959. Furthermore, again to avoid confusion with trade plates, the reversed FD series continued from 1001. Smethwick used 1 HA and 2 HA for civic cars with ordinary reversed HA issues starting at 500. Although Stoke-on-Trent did not start ordinary issues of reversed VT until March 1963, 1 VT was issued for the mayoral car in September 1959. West Bromwich issued 1 EA for its mayoral car in May 1959, the only reversed EA mark they issued. Files in the National Archives reveal that Dudley and West Bromwich sought special authorisation from the Ministry of Transport and Civil Aviation to issue 1 FD and 1 EA respectively out of sequence; Stoke-on-Trent does not appear to have sought that authority to issue 1 VT and it is not clear whether Croydon and Smethwick did with their marks.

The VT code was issued by Stoke-on-Trent and 1 VT is its mayoral car. This number was specially issued early for this purpose in September 1959 – 2 VT was not issued until March 1963.

Of even greater interest from a registration perspective are the mayoral (well mainly provostal actually) registrations with the number 0. Eight such marks exist and all are on official council cars – the number 0 has never been used on its own on an ordinary registration. These 0 marks are G 0 (Glasgow), HS 0 (Renfrewshire the mark has now

This is the only English official council with a 0 registration – all others are Scottish issues. LM 0 is the car used by the Lord Mayor of the City of London.

passed to Eastwood), LM 0 (City of London), RG 0 (Aberdeen), S 0 (Edinburgh), SY 0 (Midlothian), V 0 (Lanarkshire the mark has now passed to Glasgow) and VS 0 (Greenock). I would very much like to know more about the history of these numbers, but have only managed to find out about G 0, LM 0, RG 0 and V 0. An article in the edition of 'Motor World,' which was published in Glasgow, of 4 February 1915 reports the allocation of G 0 to a new provostal Daimler and questions whether it is a legal registration. It states that it was issued as G 1 belonged to a Mr R J Smith and, as far

The Lord Provost of Edinburgh has the number S 0. This photo was taken some time ago and the number is now on a BMW saloon. Europlate.

as the article's writer knew, no other 0 registrations had been issued. LM 0 was issued when Sir James Miller was Lord Mayor of London in 1964/5. He had previously been Lord Provost of Edinburgh from 1951 to 1954 and would have been familiar with S 0, so suggested that the City of London should also adopt a 0 registration. Wikipedia reports an interesting tale about S 0. Sir John Macdonald who died in 1919 was the original owner of S 1 and the provost of Edinburgh approached him to ask if that could be transferred to the official car. Wikipedia reports his response was "on your bike" and this was the first use of the phrase. Dictionaries of phrases, however, indicate the phrase "on your bike" dates from the 1960s, so it seems this report is incorrect. RG 0 dates from a similar time to LM 0, from July 1964 when Aberdeen took delivery of a new provostal car, an Austin Vanden Plas Princess. Previously the official car had borne DRG 1, but a third party was interested in acquiring the number and RG 0 was put on the new car. DRG 1 does still survive incidentally as a personal plate. Lanarkshire's V 0 also dates from around 1964. In a letter dated 6 November 1964 on a file in the National Archives Lanarkshire's Local Taxation Officer writes to the Ministry of Transport asking for permission to issue V 0 for the County Convenor's official car, citing Edinburgh's and Glasgow's similar marks as precedents. A handwritten note on the letter says, "Mr. McKay [the Local Taxation Officer] informed by telephone that this was a matter for himself to decide and we did not want to become involved." The circumstances behind the issuing of other "0" marks is not known.

Finally on plates for special people, in the 1950s there was an arrangement whereby the car the Prime Minister was due to travel in would always carry the plate, JUU 570, so police and other officials could recognise it. The number was swapped between different cars as necessary. Nowadays it would be considered a major security risk for the Prime Minister to have a car with a readily recognisable number and indeed for security reasons when Margaret Thatcher became Prime Minister, her husband Denis sold his distinctive number DT 3 for this reason.

CHAPTER 13 – PERSONAL PLATES

The number plate on the Singer shown will help to identify the motorist on the right of the photograph. He is Mr. Harry Tate, the well-known comedian, whose humorous skit "Motoring" is one of the cleverest burlesques of the pastime ever staged.

It is not unusual for celebrities to have their own personal plates nowadays. The first known example of this phenomenon was the music hall comedian Harry Tate who had the number T 8. This photo was taken from "The Light Car and Cyclecar" of 17 January 1915. On one occasion in 1935 two journalists spotted Harry Tate's car from its number plate and followed it. They realised he was driving erratically and signalled a police car who stopped him. Tate was charged with driving under the influence of drink and dangerous driving. He was acquitted on the first charge, but fined £12-12s on the latter.

Whilst interest in personal plates (also referred to as cherished numbers) has considerably increased in recent years, it has been possible to transfer a number in Britain ever since the introduction of vehicle registrations. This chapter looks at how the legislation relating to this has changed over the years and related matters. According to the book, "The Concise Guide to Car Numbers" by Tony Hill, proprietor of Elite Registrations, possibly the first transfer took place on 3 March 1904. This was the transfer of CR 1 by Dr Robert Lauder of Southampton from a 5hp Kimberley to an 11hp Clement.

Before 1921, the registration system was much more flexible than it subsequently became. At that time a vehicle did not necessarily normally have its registration for its life – for instance, a vehicle could be re-registered if it was transferred from one local authority area to another and often an owner changing their car would keep its number and put it on their next car. Correspondence in "Autocar" (11 and 18 June 1904) indicates that a transfer system existed. A fee of £1 is quoted as being required.

Under the heading, "Motor Registration", the "Daily Mail" of 9 April 1904 had the following story:

"Automobilists who have secured a registration number which they fancy are naturally desirous of retaining the same combination on acquiring a new motor-car and parting with the old one. Some doubt has existed, however, as to whether this is permissible, and, if so, at what cost. The Motor Union recently suggested to the Local Government Board that the owner should be at liberty to transfer his number-plate to a new motor-car on payment of a fee of five shillings, instead of the guinea which is demanded when a motor-car is registered for the first time.

"The Local Government Board has now replied, however, that the separate number which is required by the Motor-Car (sic) Act to be assigned to a motor-car "attaches to the car itself and not to the owner," and that the Board have no power to decree otherwise. They point out, however, that there is nothing to prevent an automobilist transferring the number to his own motor-car provided he pays the full fee; that is to say the old registration can be cancelled and the new motor-car registered under the old number, leaving the other owner to obtain a new number for the second-hand motor-car."

The Roads Act 1920 which came into effect on 1 January 1921 introduced many changes to the British registration system. These included a requirement that a vehicle's registration should remain with it for its life. This seems to have been taken by local authorities to indicate that they should cease carrying out transfers. Again, "Autocar" records the situation. An editorial and letters (14 and 28 May 1921) call for the reintroduction of the transfer system. One letter from a doctor bemoans the loss of his R 67

The owner of this Bentley may have LPG as their initials but more likely this car has LPG 1 as its number as it has been adapted to operate on liquified petroleum gas. This shows that all sorts of reasons could be used for choosing a personal plate.

number which had been used by his patients to recognise his car. As an aside, another reader expresses surprise at having been issued in 1903 with "such a high number as P 161"! On 19 July 1921, the Ministry of Transport issued "Information Circular No. 5" to local authorities which included the following paragraphs:

"Transfer of Identification Mark and Number

"The scheme of registration and licensing prescribed under the Finance Act 1902 and Roads Act 1920 requires that a vehicle shall retain its identification mark and number irrespective of change of ownership, etc., but strong representations have been made to the Minister by owners who, when disposing of a car, desire, usually from sentimental reasons, to transfer its identification mark and number to a new car.

"Whilst any substantial departure from normal procedure would cause serious inconvenience to Councils, and involve material expense to the Road Fund the Minister wishes, so far as practicable, to meet the expressed desire of a section of the motor owning community and will accordingly raise no objection to Councils acceding to a request for the transfer of an identification mark and registration number on payment of £5, subject to the conditions set out below. The fee of £5 has been fixed in order to cover the additional work imposed on the Council concerned and to limit the number of these exceptional cases. It will be recognised that from an administrative standpoint the transfer of identification marks and numbers from one vehicle to another is undesirable, and any request for such a transfer is presumably based upon sentimental or business grounds."

The Circular then outlines administrative procedures to effect the transfer. It goes on to say:

"Numbers cannot in any circumstances be transferred from vehicles reported to have been stolen.

"The Ministry recognises that these arrangements are extra-statutory and that it is not competent to him to direct Councils to accede to such requests for transfer, but he hopes they will co-operate, so far as is practicable. In meeting the wishes of motorists in this matter, especially as the fee of £5 will enure to the Road Fund and increase the amount

A photo of GF 21 on its original Austin 7 appeared in chapter 2. In the early 1970s this number was transferred to a Renault 6 belonging to Geoff Fitzjohn who still owns the number. – Geoff Fitzjohn.

available for road grants. It should be noted that while the representations to the Minister have been in connection with private motor cars, the arrangements set out in these paragraphs may, if desired, be applied to motor vehicles of any class."

Emphasis should be put on the use of the term "extra-statutory" to describe the concession to allow transfers. We will return to this later.

It seems that although local authorities had discretion whether to carry out transfers they invariably did. Furthermore, they seem to have worked to a set of common rules, certainly by at least the 1950s and possibly as far back as 1921. A 1975 transfer form which sets out the rules that had evolved by that time, says that a registration mark may be transferred from one vehicle to another provided neither vehicle:

"(a) is a public service vehicle (e.g. a bus)

(b) is licensed as a goods vehicle and exceeds 30 cwt unladen weight (3½ tons plated weight)

(c) is subject to customs restrictions

(d) bears a Republic of Ireland Registration mark."

It seems that public service vehicles included hackney carriages, though this could be got round by relicensing the vehicle as a private one.

An interesting reference to the restriction preventing transfers from goods vehicles can be found in Noel Woodall's book "Celebrities", published in 1962. This states, "To the uninitiated it is difficult to appreciate the lengths a car owner will to go to for possession of his OWN (sic) plates. It has been known for a commercial vehicle to be bought especially for its number, then a private body is fitted so that as a private vehicle the number can be transferred to the eagerly waiting executive's Bentley."

Ministry of Transport files in the National Archives, however, seem to indicate transfers involving goods vehicles or ones which had been goods vehicles in the past were not allowed. A note in a file reveals that the goods vehicle restriction was introduced in 1934 – "The decision to do this followed a resolution by the Chairman of the Traffic Commissioners which was accepted by the Department." This included "dual-purpose vehicles", i.e. estate cars, even if they were never taxed as goods vehicles. As estate cars were increasingly being used as family cars, this restriction seemed somewhat anomalous and in May 1962 transfers off them were permitted provided they had

OHV 1 is not the original number on this McLauglin-Buick Mpdel 40 Special. It has been transferred onto it at some time in its life. The Buick is a 1938 car, but OHV was not issued by East Ham until May 1959. The number was no doubt chosen for this car as it has a Buick Fireball Eight Overhead Valve engine.

never been licensed as hackney carriages or for goods purposes. The reason for excluding public service vehicles and vehicles which had been licensed for goods use as the administration of the record systems for such licensing was based on registration records.

It appears that "vehicles subject to customs restrictions" are those temporarily bought into the country and registered with the Qx marks referred to in chapter 10. Although transfers of Irish Republic numbers were precluded, there are some on the British system possibly dating from the time when vehicles imported from the Republic kept their numbers and some of these had been transferred off their original vehicles. This issue is looked at further in Chapter 9 on Irish registrations.

Registrations could only be transferred between two vehicles belonging to the same keeper. Whilst this might appear to have precluded the sale of registrations separately from their vehicles, in practice when a registration was sold to a new owner this restriction was avoided by registering the recipient vehicle in the same name as the donor vehicle to enable the transfer to take place. Pending acquisition of a new vehicle it was possible to hold a number on a retention certificate, thus saving the need to own two vehicles at once. Apart from the addition of 40p when value added tax was introduced on 1 April 1973, the transfer fee remained at the same £5 rate until 1977.

There was no requirement for vehicles to be taxed, only that they had to be in existence. Whilst generally there was no system for the inspection of donor vehicles to verify their existence, it seems that in some cases such inspections were carried out by the police. As a result of this lack of inspection, when personal plates started becoming more popular there appears to have been abuse of the system whereby numbers were transferred off vehicles which had been scrapped but whose logbooks had not been destroyed.

Between 1955 and 1962 it was possible to apply to a local authority to have a previously issued number reissued for the sum of £5, provided the authority was satisfied that the vehicle originally bearing it had been scrapped or permanently exported. There is some evidence that some authorities would

The Automobile Association used the £5 reissue scheme to obtain AA 1, 2 and 3. AA 2 is photographed on a preserved 1918 Chater Lea patrol motorcycle, but the number now appears to be on a retention certificate.

reissue numbers on payment of £5 earlier than 1955, but it is not known how common this practice was. The provision was discontinued in 1962 as it was frequently costing more than £5 in staff time to find a suitable number to meet an individual's request. Many of the marks comprising one or two letters followed by one or two numerals are £5 reissues from this period.

Although numbers could not be transferred off commercial vehicles, it was possible to put a £5 reissue onto one, but once this had occurred the mark could not subsequently be "moved on". The Ministry of Transport files in the National Archives reveal that it was not unusual for complaints to be made about this. The Alan Firmin Company, a haulage company that still trades in Kent, used to regularly obtain £5 reissues from Cornwall who issued "AF" marks for their new lorries. The Archives files reveal that when £5 reissues were abolished and their supply of new "AF" marks dried up, they requested permission to transfer their existing marks to new lorries, but this was not allowed, of course. Despite their raising the issue with their MP and a meeting being held involving the Ministry, their MP and company representatives, they were not able to get authority to do this.

Perhaps surprisingly, when year letters were introduced no restriction was introduced to prevent using the transfer system to make a car look newer than it was.

By 1976 transfers were becoming very frequent, but at £5.40 a time the government was actually making a loss on each one! Furthermore, number dealers were scouring scrapyards throughout the country for "any old wreck" which they could sell the number off and sometimes

Until 1977 it was possible to use the transfer system to make a car look newer than it was. The FB Vauxhall Victor was manufactured from 1961 to 1964 and this one was first registered in July 1962, but had a 1965 Denbighshire number, CCA 1C, transferred onto it.

numbers were being obtained by fraudulent activity. As it was felt transfers were taking up a disproportionate amount of staff time, on 2 August 1976 two civil service unions imposed a ban on further transfers. They argued that transfers were illegal as the Motor Car Act 1920 provided that vehicles should keep their numbers for their whole lives and the transfer facility was extra-statutory. This strike put a stop to most transfers, though some local authorities continued carrying them out where both vehicles had local authority logbooks, i.e. their details had not yet been entered onto the DVLC computer. The strike resulted in intensive lobbying by dealers and personal plate owners for the return of transfers. It was at this time that the Registration Numbers Club, a club that represents the interests of personal plate owners, was formed.

In November 1976 the dispute was resolved and new rules were introduced for transfers. Also, the government introduced legislation to permit transfers, thus at last making them no longer extra statutory. Retention certificates were abolished; all existing numbers on certificates having to be put onto vehicles between 26 November 1976 and 10 January 1977, the date when transfers would again be permitted. Many dealers with numbers held on retention certificates had to hold "closing down sales" to get rid of their stock for whatever price they could obtain. The following changes were made to the transfer rules:

1. Registrations could only be transferred off vehicles which were taxed or the subject of an application to tax and, where appropriate, MOT'd.
2. Donor vehicles had to be inspected before a transfer could take place to verify the chassis number.

3. A transfer could only take place after the donor vehicle had been registered in its keeper's name for at least nine months.
4. Numbers could not be transferred to and from motorcycles and mopeds.

Also, the transfer fee was raised to a VAT-exempt £50 from 1 March 1977.

A couple of modifications were subsequently made to the rules. Transfers from motorcycles and mopeds to four-wheeled vehicles were allowed, but "vice versa" transfers remained prohibited (They are now permitted). On 1 March 1978 the nine-month qualifying period before a transfer was allowed was reduced to three months. Whilst transfers were again permitted, number dealers still felt the rules were unduly harsh and campaigned for further changes to be made. The government responded by indicating it would review the transfer rules and issue a consultation paper which, after some delay, was eventually published.

Following the consultation exercise new rules were introduced on 10 January 1983. The main changes related to the vehicles eligible to have their numbers transferred off them. From now on, numbers could only be transferred off and onto vehicles subject to testing, MOT, PSV or HGV, i.e. eligibility was extended to

The JM 265 number on this Ferrari 250LM would almost certainly been a £5 reissue. When this photo was taken this car belonged to Jack Maurice of Gosforth, Newcastle who campaigned it with this number. The car has an interesting history. It was displayed at the 1964 Motor Show and then bought by Ron Fry (of Fry's Chocolate) who put the registration RON 54 on it and used it mainly in hillclimbs from 1964 to 1966. It was then displayed at the 1966 Motor Show and subsequently sold to Jack Maurice who put JM 265 on it and continued to campaign it till 1975. It has now reverted to the RON 54 number and has become known as "The RON 54 Ferrari."

public service vehicles and heavy goods vehicles. Conversely transfers off vehicles not subject to testing, e.g. tractors and milk floats, were immediately halted. This caused an outcry, especially as the consultation paper had not hinted at this. As a result the government conceded a "period of grace" from 5 April to 30 September 1983 for transfers off such vehicles.

Other changes introduced were:

1. Transfers between vehicles with different registered keepers were permitted. To prevent fraud, both parties had to sign the application form in such cases.
2. The requirement to have had a donor vehicle registered in the keeper's name with that registration for at least three months was dropped. From now on the only requirement was that a further transfer could not take place till a registration document had been received.

3. In certain circumstances transfers would be permitted off vehicles which could not be taxed as they had failed their MOT tests.
4. Whereas previously a mark could not be transferred if a vehicle was stolen and not recovered, transfers could now take place in such circumstances after a five-year waiting period (this period has now been reduced to six months).
5. Inspections would no longer be required when there had been a previous inspection and the transfer involved the same keeper.

The transfer fee was again increased, this time to £80. At the same time a decision was made to "call in" all local authority issued marks which had not yet been put onto the DVLC computer. Owners of these had to claim their marks before 30 November 1983 or they could lose their rights to them. This issue is looked at in more detail in chapter 11 on age-related re-registrations.

When Q-prefix registrations were introduced on 1 August 1983 vehicles bearing these were added to the eligibility exclusions.

The first DVLC (as it was then called) Auction was held at Christie's on 14 December 1989. To publicise the sale a number of framed plates were displayed at the sale and this is one of them. 1990 RR sold for a £7,500 hammer price. The number is now on a Mercedes-Benz Estate, not a Rolls-Royce, but at one time it was borne by a diesel Vauxhall Astra!

Until 1989, apart from the £5 reissues, all personal plates were numbers which had been issued ordinarily. Legislation was, however, introduced to allow DVLC to sell registrations and on 14 December 1989 the first DVLC auction was held at Christie's, London. 74 marks were sold with over £1¼ million being raised for the Exchequer. The highest hammer price was £160,000 for 1 A (buyer's

On 1 October 1990 DVLC started its scheme for selling numbers by telesales. This enabled this Chinese takeaway owner to acquire H18 WAH to advertise his business. The numbers on the plate are not legally spaced – no doubt to emphasise the 8 as 8 is considered a lucky number by Chinese people. – Bernard Minton.

premium of 10% and VAT then at 15% has to be added to this figure to obtain the total price). Auctions have been held regularly since then although auctions are no longer run by "prestige" auctioneers such as Christie's. Jumping somewhat ahead in time, in October 2008 the first online auction was held and these are now held four times a year and conventional live auctions are held five times a year.

As recounted in chapter 7, on 1 October 1990 telesales of the held back H1 to 20 marks commenced and the range of marks sold under this scheme was gradually extended as is explained in that chapter. This scheme was subsequently extended to include online sales and nowadays they are sold only online. When current system marks were introduced in 2001, certain current system marks were made available for sale online as chapter 8 explains.

On 1 April 1991 the requirements for vehicle inspections were further reduced so now only a proportion are inspected. On 1 April 1992 retention certificates, which enable one to "store" a number whilst changing cars, were reintroduced

. CHAPTER 14 – HOW TO BUY A PERSONAL PLATE

The commonest reason for acquiring a personal plate is to have your initials. This photo shows John Weeks, a Europlate member, with 3889 JW. In case you are wondering why there are two cars with the same number, this photo was taken on the day when John bought a new car. John Weeks

Maybe reading about vehicle registrations in this book has encouraged you to have a personal plate of your own. If so, this chapter will help you find one. It might be a statement of the obvious, but the first thing you need to do is to decide roughly what you want. I would emphasise the "roughly" as generally it is not wise to set out just wanting, say ABC 123 as when you decide you want a particular number you could well find the vehicle it was on has been scrapped, so it would not be available, but even if the vehicle has not been scrapped, the owner of that number (assuming you can trace them) might not wish to part with the mark, although you might offer more than it is worth.

Most people wanting a personal plate opt for a one containing their initials. If you have three initials, it is generally possible to find something matching them, unless one of them is I, Q or Z. If you have just two, your choice is potentially limited to 19,998 combinations, but in practice it will be a lot less as many vehicles bearing your letter pair, especially the forward ones will have been scrapped. To get round this sometimes people might add an X to make three letters, e.g. John Smith might opt for a JSX combination. People with four initials have to choose a suffix or prefix mark to get all of them on a plate, of course.

When you have a short name, you can have that on a plate, e.g. DON, SUE or TOM for first names or COX, LAU or ROE for surnames. Names with four letters can be

accommodated as suffix or prefix marks, e.g. AND-Y, GUN-N, J-OHN, ROS-E or T-ONY and five-letter ones can be "wrapped around" an age identifier in the current system, e.g. AA-RON, CA-ROL, JA-MES, PA-TEL or WE-NDY. It is sometimes possible to get a whole name onto a plate, e.g. BOB 8Y, D1 ANA, DAV 1D, JUL 1E, PAR 15H or WAT 5ON. In the case of my surname, Harrison, as it comprises eight letters it cannot be put onto a plate but HAR

F1 LBY sold for £3,000 at a DVLA auction in March 1991 and was bought by Alan Filby of Bedford. Mr Filby is fortunate in being able to get his surname on his plate.

150N is a near equivalent and this was issued by Chelmsford in 1974 and is now on a modern car, no doubt belonging to somebody with the surname Harrison, though sadly not myself.

At this stage it is worth mentioning that some numbers can be read as letter or vice versa, e.g. 0 = O, 1 = I or L, 2 = R or Z, 3 = E, 4 = A, 5 = S, 6 = C or G, 7 = T, 8 = B, 9 = P, 12 = R and 13 = B. More imaginative people might be able to make letters out of other numbers, but unless it is reasonably obvious what a plate "spells" it is not likely to have resale value and doctoring characters or misspacing them is illegal.

Should you have any doubt about which football team this motorist supports, it is on the script at the bottom of the plate. This is an example of a number sold direct by DVLA. The spacing of the plate is, of course, illegal – the space should be between the "4" and the "N". The photo also shows how a "4" can be substituted for an "A".

There are plenty of options as well as initials or names. You can have a plate related to your profession such as one with DOC or LAW in it. Football fans can go for something relating to their team like AFC (Arsenal) or WHU (West Ham United). Some people choose a number reflecting the pet they own, such as DOG or CAT. You might choose something based on the car you drive like BMW or JAG, but do remember that you might not always be driving the same make of car before opting for this! Some people like to be rude – the two rudest marks in circulation are probably FU 2 and PEN 15. Others opt for a number with no real meaning – they choose something that just looks nice or just something to disguise the age of their car. There are many different reasons for choosing personal plates, so really it is up to you to decide what you want.

Having chosen roughly what you would like, you then need to do some research. There are different types of number available and what you go for will depend on what you are after and what your budget is. I will go through the various types in turn:

YEARLESS MARKS

These are, of course, available in forward and reversed formats. Forward marks normally attract a premium over reversed ones. Prices range from several hundred pounds for three letters which are unlikely to be anybody's initials, e.g. containing U or X, and three nondescript numbers, not say 300 or 777, to well into six figures for one letter or two letters likely to be somebody's initials and a number one.

It is not unusual to have a personal plate relating to the make of car. This Porsche 911 bears THE 911Y, an ordinary issue from 1982 from Sheffield. Because they can be displayed on Porsche 911s, marks with "911" numbers attract a premium. The plate with a red background is, of course, totally illegal!

SUFFIX AND PREFIX MARKS

Unless they spell a name or similar, most people would only want a prefix mark with a low or "nice" number, e.g. 300 or 555. Particularly suffix numbers, but both suffix and prefix numbers would nowadays generally be recognised as being personal plates, so nobody is likely to think you are driving an old car.

This is an example of a current system registration used as a personal plate, one bought direct from DVLA. CO03 PER won the prize for the best current system plate at the rally to mark the centenary of the Motor Car Act 1903 at Woburn Abbey in 2003.

CURRENT SYSTEM MARKS

Generally people use personal plates to disguise the age of their car, but if you want your neighbours to know you have a new car, you can choose to buy a number with the current age identifier. Current system numbers also have the advantage that they have five letters, so can be used if you want to display a five-letter word or the initials of a couple.

NORTHERN IRELAND MARKS

As these are still being issued they are generally cheaper than mainland suffixless registrations. If you are looking for a combination with an I or Z in, a Northern Ireland mark is pretty well your only option (though Z is used in the letter trio in current system marks too). Ordinarily issued marks are now in the LLL nnnn format, but shorter numbers are available, either older issues or ones sold by DVLA. Generally only Northern Ireland combinations are available, so if you are looking for a particular Irish number check whether it was issued in the North or South. A very few Irish Republic marks are on the British system, so if you are looking for a combination issued in the Republic you might just find what you are after, but your chances of doing so are remote.

If you are looking for a specific letter combination or one or two such combinations, e.g. your initials or your football team's initials, you need to find out whether it has been issued. For yearless and Northern Ireland combinations, the code list at the end of the book will help you find

This is a DVL-Northern Ireland auction mark used as a personal plate. The forward control Land Rover was known as the Land Rover 101 as its wheelbase was 101 inches and it was only supplied to armed forces, not for civilian use. Thus MIL 101 is an ideal registration for this "demobbed" example.

out if a particular code has been issued. If you are looking for an ABC mark, you will see that BC was issued by Leicester and Leicester issued up to 400 JBC. Thus, ABC will have been issued in both forward and reversed formats, so somebody wanting a yearless ABC mark will have to find one that has been issued previously. You will not be able to buy one without a year letter at a DVLA auction, as only previously unissued numbers are sold at these. Similarly, if you are looking for an AB, you will see from the code list that no reversed ABs were issued normally by Worcestershire. Thus, potentially 9999 AB marks could be auctioned, so unless you particularly desire a forward combination, a DVLA auction would be a good place to buy one. Finding out if a combination with a year letter has been issued before is more difficult than finding out if a yearless one has using the code list. "Where's it from? When was it issued?" (See bibliography) gives details of what has been issued up to L-prefix, but for more recent series you would have to get hold of a Glass's Guide which would not be particularly easy, though as DVLA has a wide range of prefix marks for sale, few are likely to need to do this.

When buying a personal plate it is important to know about their values. Like all commodities, the value of registrations depends on the law of supply and demand. The supply is, of course, how many are available with that letter combination. The demand generally depends on the desirability of the letters. Letters which are a common set of initials, e.g. with the last letter a H, J or R which are common surname initials, attract a premium, but combinations which are unlikely to be anybody's initials, e.g. if they contain a U or X, will generally sell quite cheaply. The desirability of the number has to be factored in too – short or nice numbers increase the value of a mark and a number 1 is, of course, the most desirable number.

You have probably seen dealers' advertisements on the web and in newspapers and magazines and you might think that that is where to start looking. In many cases you would be better starting to look on the DVLA Sale of Marks website, www.dvlaregistrations.direct.gov.uk. Here you will find the prefix and current system marks held back for sale, referred to in chapters 7 and 8, available on line. The prefix marks have been on sale for a long time and many of the more desirable

combinations have now been sold, but you might find something that suits you and some prices are cheap with marks starting at £250. This includes the £80 transfer fee – prices in dealers' adverts normally do not include this.

The DVLA also holds auctions several times a year. Some are online auctions and others are held in

If you go to a DVLA Auction, this is how the scene might look. This photo was taken at a special auction related to the Olympic Games held at City Hall, London in July 2012 (the backdrop to this sale is the River Thames). 97 H, the featured lot, sold for £7.100.

venues throughout the country, though you do not have to attend the sale as you can bid by phone, post or on the internet. The marks offered in the "live" sales tend to be of a higher quality than those in the online sales. The prices of marks sold in previous sales can be found on the DVLA Sale of Marks website and before bidding in an auction, particularly at a "live" sale, it is important you see what similar marks have sold for in recent sales. The online sales work in a similar fashion to eBay – you give your maximum bid, but you only pay one increment above the next-highest bidder's maximum, e.g. if you have said your maximum bid was £500, but the next-highest bidder's maximum was £250, you will pay £260. In a "live" sale you have to be especially careful to set yourself a maximum limit and not get carried away paying over the odds – there is likely to be a similar mark in a future sale (and you can always request that one be put into a future sale as DVLA normally tries to meet such requests). Prices at any type of auction, whether for houses, cars, antiques or whatever tend to be a bit unpredictable as, if two people really want a lot, it can go for a lot of money whereas, if there is little interest, it can go quite cheaply. The same applies for registration auctions. Quite a few bidders at auctions are dealers who go for the cheaper lots which they can sell on at a premium. When you are bidding at a

DVLA auction bear in mind the bid price is subject to a buyer's premium (at the time of writing 8%) and value-added tax, plus the £80 assignment fee, so factor this in when you are deciding your bid limit. The sale prices quoted for previous marks sold on the DVLA Sale of Marks website do not include these "additions".

Particularly if you are looking for a mark in a series that has been issued before, a dealer might be the best place to buy a number. Dealers' advertisements appear in the "Sunday Times", the "Daily Telegraph" on Saturdays, in motoring magazines, etc and dealers invariably have websites. Spend time trawling through these adverts and get a feel for what would be reasonable to pay for what you want. Many dealers are willing to haggle, so do not necessarily agree to pay the advertised price. Sometimes selling a personal plate will have it placed with more than one dealer and the different dealers will be advertising it at different prices, so if you see a mark you like google it and see if another dealer is offering it more cheaply (and you may be able to play one dealer off against another to reduce the price). If the dealer is selling a mark which they have recently bought in an auction, you can look at the DVLA Sale of Marks website and see what they paid for it, but do not forget to add the buyer's premium and VAT. If you want to haggle, this information will, of course, be very useful. Dealers often advertise prefix marks and sometimes current-system ones which are also on the DVLA website and their price will be higher as they need to make a profit (but they also have to have a mark-up

Some number dealers offer replacement marks received after transfers as cheap numbers. ANC 500A is such a number which provides an appropriate mark for a company called ANC.

as their staff will help you make sure the transfer proceeds smoothly). Prices quoted by dealers normally exclude the £80 transfer fee, whereas those on the DVLA website include this, so be aware of this. Some dealers offer marks, mainly ones with year suffixes, but sometimes ones with prefixes, which have been issued as re-registrations quite cheaply priced. If one of these meets your requirements and you consider the price reasonable, go for it, but bear in mind you are probably unlikely to be able to sell it on in future. There are three trade associations for number plate dealers, the Cherished Number Dealers Association (CNDA), the Cherished Number Guild and the Institute of Registration Agents and Dealers (MIRAD). If you are dealing with a firm which is a member of one of these groups, you have greater security should something go wrong with the buying process. If the firm you are dealing with is not a member of one of these bodies, be careful, especially if it is not a long-established company. It would be worthwhile having a solicitor or other professional hold the payment on your behalf and release it to the vendor once the mark has been assigned to your vehicle,

Sometimes individuals sell their numbers themselves as this saves them the cost of paying a dealer's commission. It is not unusual for such individuals to over-value their numbers, so be a bit wary of this. There is a risk that somebody runs off with your money when you are buying from an individual. Again it might be worthwhile a solicitor, etc holding the payment till the transaction is completed

Sometimes people just opt for a number which takes the year letter off their car. The Jeep Grand Cherokee featured in this 1999 Chrysler Jeep publicity photo has no significance. Frequently numbers featured in car adverts are fictitious, but this one is genuine, issued by Cardiff in April 1961. Chrysler Jeep

Although at the beginning I advised that it is not a good idea to decide that you want a particular number, there is one exception to this rule. If the number has not been issued before you can apply to DVLA for it to be offered in an auction. For example, if you are John Peter Smith and because you live at 123 Acacia Avenue you would like to have JPS with the number 123, you could ask DVLA to put 123 JPS into an auction (at the time of writing JPS 123 has been auctioned, but 123 JPS has not). DVLA is generally happy to meet such requests, though you may have to wait a little while for your chosen mark to be put into a sale. The online sales particularly feature such requested marks. To take one example, a recent online sale featured GPX 750R which sold for its £200 reserve, so clearly there was only one person interested in buying it. This would almost certainly have been requested by the owner of a Suzuki GPX 750R motorcycle who wanted the perfect plate for their machine.

Novelty numbers such as this JU57 LAF (JUST LAUGH) are difficult to value as there are no similar numbers to compare prices with

It would be useful if I briefly mention what I call "novelty numbers". These are number which spell words, nicknames, etc. These are quite difficult to value as, unlike ordinary numbers, it is not possible to cite comparable numbers for valuation purposes. My advice is to get an overall feel for what number plates sell for and then decide whether you are comfortable with what is being asked for the mark. To give an example of how these marks' prices are unpredictable, in 1996 I was at a DVLA auction when such a mark, P1 NKY, was being sold and it fetched £23,100. I was sitting close to one of the largest dealers and I said to him, "If someone came to you and said they wanted to sell P1 NKY, what would you advertise it for, £4,000?" "No, £3,995," he replied. We both recognised the number had sold for several times what we would have expected it to. This not only shows now such novelty numbers can be difficult to value, but also the phenomenon I mentioned earlier, that auction prices can be unpredictable.

Some dealers say that buying a personal plate is an investment. I bought my personal number, 3890 RF, on a 1960 Lambretta scooter for £18 whilst at college and ran it for three and a half years and the number is now worth over £2,000, so you might expect me to agree. It is not that simple, however. There are costs in owning a personal plate, the £80 transfer fee each time you change your vehicle and, if you sell your mark through a dealer which most people would, you would need to pay their commission, so this would eat into your profits. Also, like commodities such as art or antiques, personal numbers go up in value when the economy is booming, but down in a recession, but it is in times of recession that people are more likely to want to raise cash by realising their investment. Cheap numbers like the prefix and current-system marks offered on the DVLA Sale of Marks website generally do not have much resale potential, so really buy one of these because you want it and can afford it. Mid-range numbers have a reasonable prospect of getting your money back if you keep them for a while, but really you have to buy towards the higher end of the marked to stand a chance of making a profit, e.g. a two-letter mark with one or two numbers or a three-letter one with a number 1 and a reasonable set of initials. If you are considering buying a personal plate in whatever price range, it makes sense to get it at a reasonable price and not pay too much. To do this you need to research the market properly, as I have said. If you do not pay over the odds for your number, you are more likely to be able to get your money back on it or even make a profit when you come to sell it.

CHAPTER 15 – TRADE PLATES

Overland cars gained a reputation for ruggedness and performing stunts like this added to this reputation. Overlands were made in Stockport and this is a Stockport General Identification Mark. This picture from the 'Motor Trader' of 17 November 1920 shows an Overland leaping two five-foot hurdles near the White City Stadium. Stockport's General Identification Marks originally comprised DB followed by a single letter and a serial number, but when the whole alphabet had been used, two letters were used in a sequence AA, AB, AC, etc.

Trade plates allow manufacturers and dealers to drive untaxed vehicles on public roads. These can, of course, include new unregistered vehicles. There have been a number of changes in their format over the years.

1904-1920 – The civil servants drafting the Motor Car Act in 1903 were sufficiently far-sighted to include provision for motor manufacturers and traders to have trade plates or general identification marks (GIMs) as they were initially called. The only rule the Local Government Board made about their format was they had to start with the code letter or letters of the local authority issuing them followed by a mixture of letters and numbers and to be of different colours than normal plates. I have spent (wasted?) many hours researching these in old motoring magazines. Whilst some information about them is available from surviving local authority records, newspaper and magazine articles, etc., most information comes from old photos. I must apologise to the various bookshops and autojumblers whose stock I have used as lending libraries to look for relevant photos!

The commonest format for GIMs was the authority's code letter(s), one or more letters denoting the user and a number indicating the number of the GIM. Thus, a user who typically had five GIMs would have numbers 1 to 5. Hampshire and Birmingham are examples of authorities who used this format. Some authorities adopted the reverse of this format, such as London and Surrey, i.e. the serial formats

The Wolseley factory was in Birmingham and its general identification marks comprised an "O", Birmingham's registration code, followed by "WY", a mnemonic for "Wolseley" and a serial number. Wolseley obviously had a lot of GIMs as photos of serial up to 88 exist.

quite often the letter(s) indicating the user were mnemonic, e.g. the GIMs used by the Wolseley Company in Birmingham commenced O-WY followed by a serial number. A third format was the authority's code, a letter or letters, usually the first letter of the authority, and a serial number. Bradford (AK-B), Warrington (ED-W) and Westmorland (EC-W) are examples of authorities that used their initial letters. Examples of authorities using other letters were Kent with D-G, Leeds with U-M and Liverpool with K-A. Confusingly, Manchester had N-MR, but adjoining Salford

Warrington's GIMs comprised "ED", Warrington's registration code, followed by a "W" for "Warrington" and a serial number

had BA-MR, so probably "MR" did not stand for "Manchester", but more likely "Motor" or "Manufacturer".

I am only aware of three contemporary colour pictures of GIMs, so information on colours is limited, but some information has been gleaned from sources such as contemporary magazine articles. White on red or scarlet was popular - Buckinghamshire, Cornwall, Coventry, Derby, Derbyshire, Glasgow, Gloucester, Gloucestershire, Hull, Leeds, Midlothian and Somerset all adopted these colours. London and Wexford's were red on white. Nottingham's were black on yellow and Warwickshire's grey on black. Westmorland users apparently had a choice of red, green or blue plates! GIMs seem to have normally been supplied by the user, so were not always in the official colours. Also, sometimes the letters and numbers were transposed – this was particularly so with Coventry's GIMs which were supposed to have the letter(s) denoting the user before the plate number, but some users, including Humber who had letter "D", put their number first, e.g. the official format would require DU.D.3, but the plate would actually be displayed as DU.3.D.

It is important to be aware that sometimes in old photos pre-1921 GIMs can be mistaken for more modern format ordinary plates. One such example which features in some old Rolls-Royce Company photos is NMR 8. Another example is Birmingham-issued OAY 3 on an Alldays and Onions.

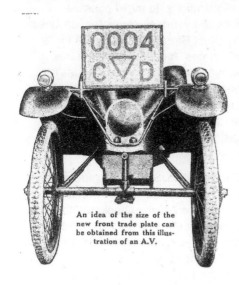

An idea of the size of the new front trade plate can be obtained from this illustration of an A.V.

This picture from "Light Car and Cyclecar" of 8 January 1921 shows how impractically large the 1921-2 format of general identification mark/trade plate was. The AV cyclecar was manufactured by Ward and Avey Ltd of Teddington.

1921-1922 – It seems that each authority having its own GIM format caused confusion and a common format was introduced in 1921. The "GIM" name was still used. They comprised a serial number starting at 0001 above the authority's code letter(s) and had red characters on a white background. The front plate included a triangular licence holder. The plates were 14½" x 10 $^{27}/_{32}$". If an old photo with a 1921-22 format GIM is found, it is, of course, very easy to give it an approximate date. From now on trade plates were officially supplied – apart from trade plates and nowadays diplomatic plates, all other British number plates have always been user supplied.

1923-1969 – Now the term "trade plate" had reached common parlance and from 1923 they were officially called that. The problem with the

A Worcester (FK code) general trade plate. Europlate.

1921-22 format GIMs was they were just too big to be practical. Also, the authorities wanted to introduce two types of trade plate, general and limited. The new plates were the same size as conventional number plates. General trade plates were white on red and limited ones red on white. The licence holder on general trade plates was rectangular and on limited ones, triangular. As

Usually trade plates had the authority's one- or two-letter code, but for reasons which are not clear West Bromwich whose code was EA used AEA. 52 AEA is a general trade plate. Reg Wilson.

When Kirkcaldy Burgh became a registration authority it issued trade plates in this format. This was the first general trade plate issued by the authority. Reg Wilson.

might be anticipated, there were tighter restrictions on the use of limited trade plates as their cost was less – remarkable though it might seem today, when first introduced they could not be used on Sundays. Both types of plate comprised a number with three or four digits and the authority's one or two code letter(s). The front plate had a licence holder above it. A few authorities used more than one or two letters, Norfolk (EVF), West Bromwich (AEA), Kirkcaldy (A-AXA), Coatbridge (B-AXB), Solihull (B-*XC), Luton (B-*XD), and Torbay (F-*XF). Norfolk used EVF after trade plate 999 PW had been issued. As 1 to 999 with its other three codes had been used for ordinary registrations, to avoid possible confusion, EVF was chosen, following on from its last yearless series for suffixless registrations, reversed EPW. I do not know why West Bromwich used AEA for its

trade plates. A consequence of this, however, was that ordinary issues in reversed AEA unusually started at 201 AEA, not 1 AEA. The other codes resulted from the creation of new registration authorities in the 1960s, of course.

1970 ONWARDS – Again trade plates reverted to a single format with red characters on a white background with a triangular licence holder on the front plate. The establishment of the Driver and Vehicle Licensing Centre in 1974 did not affect the format of trade plates.

From 1970 only one type of trade plate was used. 014 PS is such a plate from Zetland (Shetland). A pre-1970 limited trade plate would have looked similar to this. Hugh Petfield

FROM MAY 2013 – From 1 May 2013, when DVLA Local Offices stopped issuing trade plates and this function was taken over by Swansea, trade plates have had a new format. They are still red on white but initially comprised five numerals with lead zeroes being used if necessary. So far these all-

trade plates have been issued centrally and have been in an all-numeric format.

Having no doubt reached 99999 in mid-2018 the format of new trade plates changed to A followed by four numerals – Don MacFarlane.

numerical plates have only been issued when new plates have been required, so are being used alongside the post-1969 format ones. The abolition of the paper tax disc on 1 October 2014 also applied to the paper trade plate licence making the holder for it on the front trade plate redundant so new trade plates no longer have a licence holder.

In approximately September 2018, no doubt after trade plate 99999 had been issued, the format changed to a letter "A" followed by four numerals, then the letter "B". No doubt "C" will be commenced when B9999 is reached, etc.

To simplify matters, in writing about the format of trade plates so far I have conveniently ignored motorcycle trade plates. These have basically been in the same format as the trade plates for other vehicles, but smaller in size and since 1975 motorcycles only have had to display a rear trade plate.

The practice regarding the shape of licences on trade plates from 1923 to 1969 was slightly complicated. This is best explained initially using a list of trade plate types and licence holder shape then elaborating:

All-vehicle general trade plate	rectangular
Motorcycle general trade plate	trapezoidal
All-vehicle limited trade plate	triangular
Motorcycle limited trade plate	triangular

Two motorcycle trade plates, both issued by London. Hugh Petfield

A dealer in both cars, etc and motorcycles would have four trade plates (three after 1975); a larger "car" set and a smaller motorcycle set with the same numbers. They would only have one licence, however, and this had to be swapped between the two plates with licence holders depending what type of vehicle was being taken out. Dealers did not like doing this as it was time-consuming but it was the only way to ensure two vehicles were not being driven on one trade plate number at the same time. Whilst the licence and consequently licence holder were trapezoidal on a motorcycle trade general plate belonging to a motorcycle dealer only, to facilitate licence swapping a motorcycle trade plate belonging to a dealer in all types of vehicle was rectangular, so there were two types of motorcycle general trade plate with different shaped licence holders. It should also be noted that on a motorcycle limited trade plate the licence holder was orientated so that the licence could only be displayed sideways or upside-down! When a single type of trade plate was introduced in 1970 the licence was triangular. When all-numeric trade plates were introduced in 2013, the licence holder remained triangular-.

Low numbers are being used for current-format motorcycle trade plates (Currently all motorcycle plates seen have had numbers less than 03000).

CHAPTER 16 – MILITARY REGISTRATIONS

This image of a Daimler box car, with military registration M↑314, dates from 1916 and was taken in France near Albert. It was driving through the Australian Reserve lines at the time. – Rod Dux.

Until the outbreak of the First World War there were comparatively few military vehicles and these had civilian registrations, normally with marks from the registration authority where they were based. This continued to be the practice for home-based vehicles during the First World War, but for vehicles operated abroad various numbering systems were used depending on the theatre of war and the military unit involved. These numbers often featured a broad arrow. The biggest gap in our knowledge of the British registration system is the detail of these markings. We do, however, know that Army Service Corps vehicles had the following prefixes, A for ambulances, M for motor cars and RA, RC and RL for Red Cross ambulances, cars and lorries respectively. Also, WD indicated 'War Department'.

From September 1918 to 1921 temporary registrations were painted on certain military vehicles whilst in this country, not only on vehicles intended for use by the Expeditionary Forces, but also those of some Dominion and United States forces. These registrations were painted bright yellow with characters 5in high and 1in wide on the front and rear of vehicles and comprised a number followed by a suffix. The letters used were

A – Australian Forces

B – War Office and Air Force

BAC – British Ambulance Committee

C, CA, CB, CC, etc – War Office and Air Force

K – Canadian Forces

RX – British Red Cross

From 1921 to 1939 Army vehicles again received civilian registrations, issued by Middlesex. Blocks were used in H, ME, MG, MH, MK, ML, MT and HX. When three-letter series were used whole series were generally allocated for military vehicles, though some of these series were not fully used for military vehicles: AMP (21-999), BMM (21-999), CMM* (2-999), DMC (2-999), DMF (2-999), DMV* (2-999), EHX* (2-999), EME (2-999), EMG (2-999), EMV (2-999), FHX (2-999), FME* (2-999), FMG (2-999), FMX, GMF, GMY, HHX, HMC*, HMD, HMH*, HML, HMP, HMT, HMY, JME, JMF, JMG, JMK, JMV, JMX, PHX, PMC, PMD, PME, PMF, PMG, PMH, PMK, PML,PMP, PMT, PMV, PMX, PMY, RHX, RMC, RMD, RME, RMF,

This Talbot army lorry was registered in Middlesex in 1923. Colin Spong.

RMG, RMH, RMK, RML, RMP, RMT, RMV*, RMX, RMY* and SHX. The asterisked series were for armoured vehicles and after the Second World War were reissued to civilian vehicles. It is very unusual for British registrations to be reissued, but this is one instance when this occurred. Armoured vehicles were not, of course, sold off after the war for civilian use, whereas other vehicles, such as cars, motorcycles and lorries, were. When the latter were sold for civilian use, pre-1939 ones reverted to their original Middlesex registrations. 1939 to 1945 vehicles sold off had to be given new civilian registrations; of course, generally one for the authority where the new owner was based. Middlesex used all reversed SMD numbers for ex-military vehicles in 1947.

This is an army Vickers Tank registered in Middlesex. The ML series was commenced in 1926. Colin Spong.

From 1921 on, Royal Air Force vehicles had plates with "RAF" followed by a serial number. Royal Navy ones had RN followed by a serial number up to 9999 until around 1928. The prefix was then changed to a suffix to avoid possible confusion with ordinary Preston RN civilian numbers. Trailers had 'RN' as a suffix with numbers starting at 10000 RN. These plates had white characters on a black background and plates in these formats remained in use until the new-style military plates we will come to in a moment were introduced in 1949.

This Volkswagen car carries the form of Royal Air Force number plate used from 1921 until 1949. Europlate.

Although Army vehicles had Middlesex civilian registrations from 1921, they also had a serial number, normally painted on the vehicle's side, comprising a letter indicating its type followed by a seven-digit number. Shortly after the start of the Second World War in 1939, the practice of registering Army vehicles at Middlesex ceased and throughout the War and up to 1949, the serial number was displayed effectively as a registration number, usually on the sides of the vehicle. The numbers were used serially with the prefix changing as appropriate, i.e. there would not be two or more vehicles with the same number but different prefix letters. The prefixes used were:

This dramatic photo of a tank captain surrendering to the Italian Bersaglieri (sharp-shooting) Regiment shows the registration of the tank as T 27314. This is the format of army plate used from the beginning of the Second World War to 1949. "T" indicates a tank and 27314 is a serial number. Europlate.

A – Ambulances

C – Motorcycles and motorcycle combinations

D – Dragons (tracked towing vehicles)

F – Armoured cars

H – Tractors

L – Trucks (over ¾ ton)

M – Cars, utilities and buses

P – Amphibians

R – Rota trailers (for flame-throwing tanks)

S – Self-propelled guns

T – Tanks and carriers

V – Vans

X – Trailers

Z – Trucks (up to ¾ ton)

No prefix – Miscellaneous vehicles including road rollers, excavators, cranes and electric trucks

During the Second World War, the vehicles of several allied forces were integrated into this system. Also, Canadian Forces vehicles used this system with an additional C-prefix, e.g. CA would indicate a Canadian ambulance.

In 1949 a new format was introduced for all three services comprising two numerals, two letters and two numerals, i.e. 12 AB 34. AA to AY indicated Royal Air Force vehicles and RN Royal Navy ones. Generally, other letter pairs indicated the vehicle belonged to the Army and frequently related to the vehicle type. Pre-1949 vehicles transferred to this format were given marks in the ranges RA to RH, YA to YZ, ZA to ZC and ZR to ZY. Not all vehicles with the old-style numbers were re-registered as as late as 1955/6 some with these numbers were still being disposed of. The last number issued under

ZZ was a rare code in the 1949 to 1994 military registration system being used for Commonwealth vehicles operated in the United Kingdom. Europlate.

the previous system is thought to have been M.6279800 on a Land Rover delivered in December 1948.

This preserved 1943 Scammell Pioneer displays both its pre-1949 format military registration, H4782402 on the bonnet and its post-1949 format one, 34 YZ 71.

The system provided for some "personalised numbers". Until around 2005, 53 ER 01 to 53 ER 08 were used by 20 Squadron Royal Corps of Transport for the transportation of the Queen's baggage; ER being the royal cypher and 53 referring to the Queen's Coronation in 1953. Similarly, the Royal Signals Motorcycle Display Team, known as the White Helmets, used to have WH marks. The First Sea Lord used to have 00 RN 01 on his official car. Moving slightly away from "personalised numbers", after the Falklands War, captured Argentine vehicles were registered under this system with CV (captured vehicle) letters and at least one captured ex-Iraqi tank also received a CV mark. TP was a special code used for temporary plates, broadly similar to trade plates which had red characters on a white background.

When reflective plates were introduced, the norm for army vehicles became that purely military vehicles retained the old-format black plates whilst others had reflective plates, though practice in this respect has not always been consistent. When the armed forces became targets for Irish Republic Army terrorism, vehicles used "off base", such as those related to Army recruiting offices, changed to civilian registrations, whereas previously they had military ones. Although these vehicles have civilian registrations, for administrative purposes they are also allocated a military registration, though this is not displayed. Many leased army vehicles also now have civilian registrations.

In 1982 a significant change occurred. Military vehicles were now in most cases purchased centrally and registered in a common series. The letters now used progressed from KA though to KM. There was one exception to this; vehicles of types used just by the Royal Air Force or Royal Navy received, as appropriate, marks in the AY or RN series.

This Challenger 2 tank bears a current format army plate, DS 55 AA. Crown Copyright

In 1994 the format was changed to two letters, two numbers and two letters, i.e. AB 12 CD. It was reported at the time as this was to avoid possible confusion with Irish Republic registrations, though there are other countries with plates in the same format as the army's new one such as Holland. The series started at AA 00 AA, with AA 01 AA following, continuing through to AA 99 AA with AB 00 AA next and so on. When ZZ 99 AA is reached, AA 00 AB will follow. Pre-1994 AY and RN plates remain in use for Royal Air Force and Royal Navy special purchases.

To conclude this section, it is necessary briefly to consider the registration of military trailers. Apart from the larger trailers referred to in Chapter 19 which have an additional number plate, British civilian trailers are not separately registered, but carry the number plate of the towing vehicle. Except for Royal Navy nes which also carry the mark of the towing vehicle, military trailers are separately registered with plates in the same format as powered vehicles. Although not having their own number plates, Royal Navy trailers do, however, have serial numbers, effectively the equivalent of fleet numbers, continuing the 10000 RN series.

CHAPTER 17 – TRAILER REGISTRATIONS

Only three new number plate types have been introduced in Britain this century; four if the two types of trade plate are counted separately. The current format of plates described in Chapter 8 were introduced in 2001. The all-numeric format of trade plates described in Chapter 15 were introduced in 2013 with those beginning with a prefix following on in 2018. Brexit has seen the need for a new type of plate for larger trailers.

In many countries trailers have to be separately registered, but ever since the introduction of number plates under the Motor Car Act of 1903 in Britain trailers have carried the number of the towing vehicle. This is no longer the case for larger trailers. The background to this is slightly complicated.

As explained in Chapter 19 on International Identification Letters, there have been four conventions on international circulation; Paris in 1909, Paris again in 1926, Geneva in 1949 and Vienna in 1968. Britain has not been a signatory of the Vienna Convention until recently. Some European countries, notably Germany have been signatories of the 1968 Convention, not the 1949 one. This has not generally been a problem as the European Union treaties required mutual acceptance of documentation. With the possibility of Brexit and maybe a "no deal" one this recognition might not have continued. Britain therefore signed the 1968 Vienna Convention and this ratification came into full effect in March 2019. The 1968 Vienna Convention requires commercial trailers over 750 kg and all trailers over 3,500 kg to be separately registered and trailers not registered could be excluded from a signatory country. Thus, a need for such trailers being taken to Vienna Convention countries to be separately registered arose. The provision for this were the Trailer Registration Regulations 2018 1203) authorised by the Haulage Permits and Trailer Registration Act 2018. These Regulations came into full effect on 28 March 2019.

The need for registration only relates to trailers to be used in 1968 Convention countries. Non-display abroad will presumably be a matter for the relevant jurisdiction to enforce, but the Regulations require the plate to be displayed if the trailer is being used in Britain to travel to or from a country to which the 1968 Convention applies. Cyprus, Ireland, Malta and Spain are not covered by the 1968 Convention so it a trailer is being taken directly there, not through another country, registration is not necessary. There is an option for the owner of a non-commercial trailer over 750 kg to voluntarily register it under this scheme if they wish.

This is the layout for trailer plates set out in the Trailer Registra-tion Regulations 2019.

The format for these plates is a letter followed by seven numerals. Single-line "rectangular" plates are not permitted. Plates are white with black characters. The size of letters specified is slightly smaller than those for ordinary plates; 64 mm height compared with 79 mm. The plate is normally to be displayed on the rear of the vehicle in addition to the ordinary number plate of the towing vehicle if the trailer is being towed. The two plates should be as far apart as reasonably practical. There is also an option to display two trailer plates, one on each side of the trailer, if it is impractical to display the plate on the rear. It appears that these trailer plates are being issued in a random way with different prefix letters being allotted even when one haulier has made multiple applications at the same time.

It should be noted that drawbar trailers and semi-trailers, i.e. the trailer halves of articulated lorries, have to be tested annually, a requirement administered by the Driver and Vehicle Standards Agency. To facilitate this new trailers have an identification number, colloquially referred to as a "C number", e.g. C394883, welded on them by the manufacturer. These are more akin to chassis numbers on cars and are not number plates, but as there is the possibility that the two types of number could be confused it is useful to be aware of these.

CHAPTER 18 – CHILDREN COLLECTING CAR NUMBERS

This chapter has been jointly written with Adrian Tranmer

This is the cover of a booklet about motoring given away with "The Skipper" comic showing a boy (well actually he looks more like a man but this would not seem to be what the artist intends) collecting car numbers from a bridge over a very busy road. The one legible number, YL 1936, suggests this booklet was published in 1936.

This is an aspect of vehicle registration which is not normally mentioned in books on the subject, even though it used to be an important part out our culture. Older readers will probably be aware that in the 1950s and 60s and even earlier, children, generally boys, used to "collect car numbers". This chapter looks at the history of this practice, mainly using reports from contemporary newspapers. The practice almost dates back to the introduction of registration numbers. Under the Motor Car Act 1903, the display of registration plates became compulsory on motor vehicles used after 1 January 1904. Though not strictly relating to children collecting car numbers, this report from "The Motor Cycle" of 12 January 1904 relates to a sort of precursor to it:

HAVE YOU NOTICED IT? – It is curious what an interest the small boy takes in the number plates of any passing car or cycle. He will spot the mystic signs from afar, and shout out the numbers as you ride by. Cabmen appear especially disposed to offer facetious remarks, and even the policeman gives a meaning smile, as much as to say there is no escape now.

On 26 January 1904, however, "The Motor Cycle" did report the genesis of the practice:

NUMBER COLLECTORS - More than once recently we have noticed various small boys jot down the number of our machine in a notebook or a piece of paper as we rode by, they evidently keeping a record of every numbered car or cycle they may notice. And that reminds us that a list setting forth the index letters in alphabetical order, and the districts they represent, would doubtless be appreciated by motorists. A small card that would slip into the vest pocket should suffice for the purpose.

On 9 June 1904 a five-year old boy was killed at Lostock Hall, near Preston, by a 10hp Napier belonging to Charles Rolls and driven by William Lord of Fulham. This event was reported in "The Shields Daily Gazette" of 11 June and the "Northampton Mercury" of 17 June and probably quite a few other papers too. The stories were headlined, "A Dangerous Competition" and "New Motor Danger" respectively. Though the precise circumstances are not clear from the reports, it seems the boy was among a group of children collecting car numbers. A story with a different angle on events was reported in the "Evening Telegraph" and the "Essex Newsman" both of 10 August which told how a hit-and-run driver was convicted as the result of a Dunmow schoolboy, Oliver Caton, having taken the number, A 4931, before the accident whilst "spotting". The reports indicate that the manner in which the motorist was caught caused laughter in the court.

The Lostock Hall accident raised an issue regarding the safety of the practice. At the inquest the coroner's attention was drawn to newspapers offering prizes to children collecting car numbers and the danger this was causing to them. Captain Annesley, a passenger in the car, agreed to write to the papers concerned.

Though we have found no further reports of similar competitions in newspapers, there have been several reports of spurious rumours of such competitions. We have found details of several such non-existent competitions:

- "The Motor-Car Journal" of 8 July 1905 which talked about a non-existent competition offering a bicycle for collecting 1,000 numbers.
- A letter to the "Liverpool Echo" published on 9 September 1915 expressing concern about the dangers of children collecting numbers said one boy said he was entering a competition in which the first child to get 1,000 numbers would win a bicycle. The correspondent goes on to say, "He did not appear to know exactly why or from whom he would obtain the bicycle, but that did not abate his enthusiasm."
- In September 1919 "The Motor Cycle" reported receiving long lists of registration numbers from children with the expectation they would receive a prize although the magazine had not organised such a competition.
- The front page of the "Nottingham Evening Post" of 23 July 1924 reported a craze for collecting in that city. One boy was hoping to win a prize of a motorcycle for sending the most reports of Nottingham's AU registrations to the Guildhall, (the minimum age for riding a motorcycle was 14 at this time) and another lad hoped to win a "toy bicycle" from a city centre store, but neither competition existed.
- On 10 July 1925 the "Manchester Guardian" reported a press release (though that term might not have been used in those days) from the National "Safety First" Association reporting children were collecting numbers for non-existent competitions supposedly offered by newspapers or sweet or toy manufacturers and commenting on the resulting risks to road safety.
- "The [Hull] Mail" of 16, 17, 28 and 30 June 1927 dealt with this topic and on 17 June referred to a supposed prize of ten shillings for handing in a list of 1,000 numbers to either the Hull Guildhall or the "Mail" offices.
- On 16 June 1928 the "Manchester Guardian" reported a denial by Scotland Yard that they were running a competition for collecting car numbers.
- On 25 November 1937 the "Dundee Evening Telegraph" told of children "swarming" on to roads as the police were offering a £5 reward to the person

who discovered a supposed stolen car with a YS (one of the codes for Glasgow) registration when no such reward existed.

- The "Sunderland Daily Echo and Shipping Gazette" reported on 26 March 1938 that a boy had said that if he collected 160 GR numbers (GR was then the code for Sunderland) and took them to Palmers, a large department store in Sunderland, he would receive a pair of roller skates. A director of the firm is quoted as saying no such contest had ever been organised or even considered.

One wonders how these false stories managed to get about. Interestingly the "Nottingham Evening Post" report of 23 July 1924 reports two other examples of previous "phantom competitions", for collecting cigarette cards and tram tickets. It is noteworthy that most of these reports date from the summer – collecting car numbers was not as pleasant in the winter!

It seems strange that collecting car numbers was considered to be pursuing a dangerous pastime, but there is evidence this was the case. Perhaps health and safety concerns are older than we think. A letter in the "Nottingham Evening Post" of 25 July 1924 following up the item published two days earlier written by "MOTORIST" (at this time it was usual for letters to editors to be published under a pseudonym) said, "The number of children who swarm the roads in an endeavour to see the registration numbers is both a nuisance and a hindrance to traffic, to say nothing of the children being run over. They step out into the road regardless of oncoming traffic, and in many cases they stand in the middle of the road." "The [Hull] Mail" of 17 June 1924 reported a statement from the Hull City Coroner, Dr J Divine, drawing parents' attention to the danger run by children collecting numbers. The paper writes, "The danger of this practice, which has become increasingly prevalent in this district during the last few days, needs no emphasis, for in the eagerness to secure the numbers the children run grave risks of being knocked down and killed by following traffic". The "Manchester Guardian" article of 10 July 1925, previously referred to, said the practice of number collecting had "led to fatal results", but apart from the death of Oliver Caton in 1904 we have only been able to trace one other such accident. This comes from the "Sheffield Evening Telegraph" of 4 August 1910, though the events reported occurred in Preston. A schoolboy, Robert Brindle stepped off the pavement and stretched himself out and in doing so overbalanced and was hit by the car's mudguard whilst collecting car numbers. Interestingly, the report says he was taking part in a competition with a price of 10 shillings for the person who saw the most numbers, though no indication is given as to who was promoting the competition. It is perhaps surprising that the message given was to cease the practice, rather than simply to "do it from the pavement" safely.

The purpose of collecting numbers is unclear. Perhaps it was encouraged by parents to improve handwriting. In some instances spotters seem to have been just writing down the number of every passing vehicle – a somewhat random process. The pursuit seems to have dated back to only a few weeks after the introduction of the number plate under the Motor Car Act 1903. It is possible children had been used to collecting train numbers and, seeing car numbers, started collecting these too. In some instances there was element of game playing, e.g. trying to see who could be the first to see numbers 1 to 100 (or higher) in sequence ("Manchester Guardian" - 5 June 1945). The "Manchester Guardian" of 3 May 1934 recounts an arguably more sinister game from the report of the Bristol Methodist Temperance and Social Welfare Committee of children guessing what the last digit of the next car to pass would be and putting a ½d into a pool with the child who guessed correctly winning the pot. This strong condemnation might seem strange, but reports also in the "Manchester Guardian" of 30 May 1924 and 23 October 1930 of adults being prosecuted for the same practice perhaps explain why. A similar child betting practice was reported in the "Morning Post" in November 1923. In this game the digits of successive vehicles were added together with the winner of the pot being the one whose sum was the highest. At this time most vehicles would have had four numerals on their plates, thus ensuring a degree of fairness in this game. This report did not include the element of condemnation that the "Manchester Guardian" account did.

Many children's "spotter books" were produced after the war and these are a few examples. Mark Warren.

For the more serious spotter who wanted to know where cars came from there was a veritable "industry" producing spotters' books. Publishers Ian Allan who, of course, produced spotters books for a range of transport got in on the act with "Spotting the Number Plate" which ran through 18 editions from 1951 to 1967. There were nine I-Spy "Car Numbers" books published from 1967 to 1983, plus the very rare "I-Spy Spotting Car Numbers" published about 1950. In subsequent books after 1983 car numbers was merged with another topic, e.g. "I-Spy on the Motorway and Car Numbers" (1991), no doubt reflecting interest in the practice was diminishing. Raleigh Press of Exmouth published 14 editions of "Where's that Car from?" between 1946 and 1966 when the final edition was produced. The final edition proclaimed "Over half a million copies sold so far" on the cover – so it proved a popular seller. The Ian Allan, I-Spy and Raleigh books were the "big sellers", but others were also produced. "The Grantleigh Car Spotters Record Book" has an Austin A70 Hampshire on the cover, so would date from around 1950. As well as a code list this included pages for entering numbers seen, left blank apart from the slogan "Safety first is the Sqotters (sic) Code – know your drill and watch the road" – they obviously accepted that spotting could be safely pursued. The "Motor Spotter's Record Book" dating from around the same time also had blank pages for sightings, as well as road safety messages such as "Don't get off a bus or tram until it stops." "Where did that car come from?" probably dates from the mid-50s and was published by Munster, Simms & Co Ltd, Belfast. For those interested, such books sometimes turn up at autojumbles or on eBay.

The practice of collecting numbers seems to have died out now, no doubt displaced by technological inventions initially television and latterly computers and mobile phones with access to social media which are much more attractive to youngsters. This, however, was not the first "death" of the hobby. An article entitled "Collector's

Instinct" in the "Manchester Guardian" of 5 June 1945, states: "Swiftly the tale of numbers rose, in due sequence, until the century was passed. But before any but the most assiduous could claim their second century the days of petrol restriction were upon us. There was not enough cars on the road to make further collection worth while (sic)." The article then goes on to predict, quite wrongly, that the craze would not return after the war.

Car number collecting was a common practice so no doubt quite a few of today's elderly "celebs" will have pursued this pastime in their youth. We can conclude this chapter by saying one very well-known personality definitely did. In his autobiography, "If I Don't Write It Nobody Else Will", Eric Sykes wrote about an incident when he was collecting car numbers: "At the age of six, I decided I was going to sit at the side of a main road and take down the numbers of motor-cars for entertainment. I hoped for 50, but come dinner time the complete lack of cars and the cold wind were starting to dampen my enthusiasm. 'Allo, allo, allo.' I recognised the imposing figure of Constable Matty Lally, who was built like a full-grown water buffalo. 'What are you doing here, lad?' he asked. When I told him, he shook his head sadly and said: 'You'll get piles sitting there.' Naturally, I assumed he meant piles of motor cars."

The company Cornercroft Ltd was a major supplier of number plates and other products under the "Ace" name. This is a page from a 1950s catalogue for their GB plates.

The invention of the motor car soon raised the problem of a driver from one country wishing to take their vehicle to another one. It might be thought that this would not be a big issue for an island nation like Britain, but in 1908 3,000 British motorists passed through the ports of Calais, Boulogne and Le Havre. There were obvious potential problems of the acceptability of other countries' driving licences and construction requirements for motor vehicles and also, of course, number plates.

In 1909 a convention was held in Paris to resolve these issues. The convention agreed to accept a driver competency certificate issue by one of the signatory countries or a

E, like GB, was one of the codes agreed at the 1909 Paris Convention and has been in use ever since. The reason for the letter "E" is that Spain in French is Espagne. The car is a first series Morris Oxford. The VI code on the number plate indicates it was registered at Alavia in the province of Vitoria. Europlate.

recognised motoring association sanctioned by a signatory country granted after a driving test subject to a minimum age limit of 18. Minimum requirements were set for the construction of cars which would be permitted to circulate in other countries, e.g. two braking systems, a reverse gear for vehicles over 350 kilogrammes and a "deep-toned" horn.

Political considerations mean that sometimes ovals become obsolete. This 1950-53 Mulliner-bodied Alvis being unloaded from a ship carries an SS, Straits Settlements oval. The "S" on the number plate indicates the car is Singapore registered. Singapore ultimately became an independent republic and the letters SGP are now used there.

The convention requirement which relates to our interest is the introduction of international identification letters or ovals to be placed on the rear of the car which meant that a motor vehicle from one signatory country could circulate in another without having to be registered in the second country. The letters agreed by the convention signatories were Austria (A), Belgium (B), France (F), Great Britain (GB), Germany (D), Holland (NL), Hungary (H), Italy (I), Monaco (MC), Montenegro (MN), Portugal (P), Rumania (RM), Russia (R), Servia (SB), Sweden (S), Switzerland (CH) and United States (US). Although the United States was issued the letters US, it does not appear to have been an actual signatory to the convention as until after the Second

World War American cars brought temporarily into Britain had to carry the "Q" visitor plates described in chapter 10.

Subsequent conventions on road traffic were held in 1926 in Paris, 1949 in Geneva and 1968 in Vienna. The most significant country that is not a signatory is China. Any vehicle that is temporarily imported into China must be given a Chinese registration.

The widespread availability of hire cars means that in Britain ovals from countries outside Europe are rarely seen nowadays – two generations ago non-European ovals could occasionally be seen. Even European ovals are becoming less common as European Union motorists with a Eurosymbol on their plates do not need to carry an oval whilst

Although international identification letters should comprise black letters on a white oval, not all comply with this requirement. In Britain in the 50s and 60s, it was not unusual to see cars, especially expensive ones, with two chrome letters on the back instead of the conventional GB plate. This is a Greek example, 'GR' being the code for Greece, of a rather more ornate alternative

driving in another Union country. It should be noted that for these purposes the English, Scottish and Welsh symbols are not accepted – only the official Eurosymbol incorporating the "GB" letters is acceptable. Another arrangement similar to the European Union one relates to Canada, Mexico and the United States. Vehicles from one of these countries does not need to carry an oval in another as each state's/province's plates carries its name.

The following international identification letters are in use:

A	Austria	CAM	Cameroon
AFG	Afghanistan	CDN	Canada
AL	Albania	CH	Switzerland
AM	Armenia	CI	Côte d'Ivoire
AND	Andorra	CO	Columbia
AUS	Australia and territories	CR	Costa Rica
AZ	Azerbaijan	CY	Cyprus
B	Belgium	D	Germany
BD	Bangladesh	DK	Denmark and Greenland
BDS	Barbados	DOM	Dominion Republic
BF	Burkina Faso	DZ	Algeria
BG	Bulgaria		
BIH	Bosnia-Herzegovina	E	Spain
BOL	Bolivia	EAK	Kenya
BR	Brazil	EAT	Tanzania (Tanganyika)
BRN	Bahrain	EAU	Uganda
BRU	Brunei	EAZ	Tanzania (Zanzibar)
BS	Bahamas	EC	Ecuador
BVI	British Virgin Islands	ES	El Salvador
BW	Botswana	EST	Estonia
BY	Belarus	ET	Egypt
BZ	Belize	ETH	Ethiopia
C	Cuba	F	France

FIN	Finland	JA	Jamaica
FJI	Fiji		
FL	Liechtenstein	K	Cambodia (Kampuchea)
FO	Faroe Islands	KGZ	Kyrgyzstan
		KSA	Saudi Arabia
G	Gabon	KWT	Kuwait
GB	Great Britain	KZ	Kazakhstan
GBA	Alderney		
GBG	Guernsey	L	Luxembourg
GBJ	Jersey	LAO	Laos
GBM	Isle of Man	LAR	Libya
GBZ	Gibraltar	LB	Liberia
GE	Georgia	LS	Lesotho
GH	Ghana	LT	Lithuania
GR	Greece	LV	Latvia
GUY	Guyana		
		M	Malta
H	Hungary	MA	Morocco
HKJ	Jordan	MAL	Malaysia
HR	Croatia	MC	Monaco
		MD	Moldova
I	Italy	MEX	Mexico
IL	Israel	MGL	Mongolia
IND	India	MK	Macedonia
IR	Iran	MNE	Montenegro
IRL	Ireland	MOC	Mozambique
IRQ	Iraq	MS	Mauritius
IS	Iceland	MW	Malawi
J	Japan	N	Norway

NA	Netherlands Antilles		RKS	Kosovo
NAM	Namibia		RL	Lebanon
NAU	Nauru		RM	Madagascar
NEP	Nepal		RMM	Mali
NGR	Nigeria		RN	Niger
NIC	Nicaragua		RO	Romania
NL	Netherlands		ROK	Republic of Korea
NZ	New Zealand and territories		ROU	Uruguay
			RP	Philippines
P	Portugal		RSM	San Marino
PA	Panama		RUS	Russia
PE	Peru		RWA	Rwanda
PK	Pakistan			
PL	Poland		S	Sweden
PNG	Papua New Guinea		SD	Swaziland
PY	Paraguay		SGP	Singapore
			SK	Slovakia
Q	Qatar		SLO	Slovenia
			SME	Suriname
RA	Argentina		SN	Senegal
RB	Benin		SO	Somalia
RC	Taiwan (Republic of China)		SRB	Serbia
RCA	Central African Republic		SUD	Sudan
RCO	Congo (Brazzaville)		SY	Seychelles
RCH	Chile		SYR	Syria
RG	Guinea			
RGB	Guinea Bissau		T	Thailand
RH	Haiti		TCH	Tchad
RI	Indonesia		TG	Togo
RIM	Mauritania		TJ	Tajikistan

TM	Turkmenistan	WD	Dominica
TN	Tunisia	WG	Grenada
TR	Turkey	WL	St Lucia
TT	Trinidad & Tobago	WS	Samoa (Western Samoa)
		WV	St Vincent
UA	Ukraine		
USA	United States of America and territories	YAR	Yemen Arab Republic
		YV	Venezuela
UZ	Uzbekistan		
		Z	Zambia
V	Vatican City	ZA	South Africa
VN	Vietnam	ZRE	Democratic Republic of the Congo (Zaire)
WAG	Gambia	ZW	Zibabwe
WAL	Sierra Leone		

CHAPTER 20 – FINDING OUT MORE

If this book has inspired you to find out more about registrations, this chapter will point you to various sources of further information. Perhaps not surprisingly, the first thing I would like to mention is "1903 and all that", the quarterly newsletter I edit which deals with all aspects of registrations, e.g. history, what is currently being issued, personal numbers, etc; mainly concentrating on the British system. It is generally written in a fairly light-hearted way. This currently costs £10 per annum. If you would like to receive a sample backnumber, send a large envelope with a stamp for a 250g large letter to me at 175 Hillyfields, Loughton, IG10 2PW.

Registration Newsletter deals with more technical aspects of the British registration system, e.g. which registrations are issued during each age identifier period. It appears twice a year. Most of it is quite complicated, but having the sort of mind that can understand this type of thing I find it fascinating. Details of the newsletter can be found on www.registrationnl.webs.com.

The Registration Numbers Club holds an annual rally for its members. This photo was taken at the one held to mark the club's 40th anniversary at Temple Newsam Park, Leeds in July 2017.

The Registration Numbers Club is a club for personal plate owners and represents their interests with the government. It issues a quarterly newsletter and holds an annual rally. Its website is www.thernc.co.uk.

This book just deals with the British registration system, but every country, of course, has its own system. Europlate is an organisation set up for those who are interested in worldwide registrations. Many of its members collect actual number plates. It publishes a quarterly newsletter and every other year holds an Easter convention in Britain or Europe. The website is www.europlate.org.uk.

Every other year Europlate holds a convention where activities include a chance for those who collect plates to trade them. This photo was taken when the convention was held in the Tramway and Bus Museum in Luxembourg.

Books on registrations I would recommend are:

- The History of Motor Vehicle Registration in the United Kingdom by Les Newall (Newby Books – ISBN 9781872686325). This book complements my book in many ways. It similarly covers the British registration system, but in more detail, e.g. it gives dates of issue for all pre-1963 combinations and therefore enables one to find out dates of issue.
- Car Registration Guide by Peter Robson (Newby Books – ISBN 9781872686332). This is a pocketbook giving brief details of the British and Irish registration systems together with the systems of Britain's offshore islands.
- Car Numbers – Then and Now by Noel Woodall and Brian Heaton (Registration Publications – ISBN 0952071657). This is a "who's who" listing of personal plate owners.
- Where's it from? When was it issued? by Noel Woodall and Brian Heaton (Car Number Galaxy Publications – ISBN 0 95025377-4). This gives details of all registration combinations issued up to L-prefix.

- Motor Vehicle Registration Numbers of Great Britain 1963-1974 by Jonathan Del Mar (GH Smith Publishing – ISBN 9781526207326). This covers local authority issues with year suffixes.
- Car number Classics by Nicholas Young (Pieters and Young – ISBN 978157230460). Gives details of early issues by original English and Welsh and some Scottish and Irish ones local authorities issuing numbers under the Motor Car Act 1903 together with biographies of their owners, plus general information about the British registration system.

The website to visit if you want to look at old local authority records, e.g. to trace the history of a classic car or a personal plate you own is the Kithead Trust's one, www.kitheadtrust.org.uk. This tells you what records survive and where they can be inspected.

APPENDIX 1 - GLOSSARY

AFRL: Pronounced "afril". This is an acronym for "automatic first registration and licensing". This is the process introduced in the last few years whereby garages can register new vehicles directly with DVLA through computer links, rather than by visiting a LO.

Age identifier – For a 1963 to 2001 mark this is the letter indicating the vehicle's age and for post-2001 it is the two numerals indicating this.

Forward registration – a registration with the letters in front of the number.

Personal number – a number specially purchased by the owner or transferred off a vehicle previously owned by then. These are sometimes also referred to as **cherished numbers**.

RaV – an abbreviation for "Register a Vehicle", the system introduced in 2019 to register vehicles using computer links superseding AFRL.

Re-registration – a number given to a vehicle that has previously been registered, e.g. because it previously bore a personal plate, has been imported second-hand or is ex-military or ex-diplomatic. Until 1 August 1983, when issuing A-prefix started, the only marks issued as re-registrations were replacements for vehicles which had borne personal plates – the other categories of vehicles which now receive re-registrations would until then receive current-series marks.

Retention Certificate: A facility which enables a personal plate owner to apply to keep a number pending the sale of one vehicle and the acquisition of the next.

Reversed registration – a registration with the numbers in front of the letters.

"Select": This is a prefix of current-system registration sold from the DVLA Sale of Marks website, dvlaregistrations.dvla.gov.uk. The term is put in inverted commas as it used to be a marketing name used by the Sale of Marks Section, but it is no longer used by them. It is still used by registration hobbyists, however, as it has not been possible to think of another suitable alternative.

£5 reissue: Between 1955 and 1962 it was possible to apply to a Local Taxation Office to have a voided old number reissued at a cost of £5, so such number are referred to as £5 reissues.

APPENDIX 2 – CODE LIST: 1903 TO 2001

This is a list of the codes used for the pre-2001 system, i.e. up to the end of Y-prefix on 31 August 2001. Generally each code, apart from single-letter ones, will have been issued by a local authority up to 30 September 1974 and by a Local Vehicle Licensing Office/Vehicle Registration Office. Where local authorities have merged or LVLOs/VROs closed and a nearby office has continued to issue its numbers as local marks, this is indicated. An asterisk adjacent to a code in the left-hand column indicates that some "yearless" combinations with that code have subsequently been (or will soon be) used as age-related re-registrations.

The third column is the last known suffixless issue by the local authority or a LVLO which took over issuing its marks. Thus, this includes re-registrations which will have been issued after the authority went on to year letters or in some cases by the successor Local Vehicle Licensing Office. Except for "999" or "9999" numbers, these are the last known ones issued and possibly slightly higher numbers may have been issued and in some instances higher "specials", numbers issued on special request, may also have been issued. Where an authority issued reversed registrations, if both two- and three-letter reversed combinations were used, the highest for both series is indicated; where only one type was used there is only one entry. As Northern Ireland issues have progressed through two-letter forward combinations, two-letter reversed combinations, then forward three-letter and four-numeral combinations, an entry in the third column just in the format 9999 LL indicates that for that code three-letter combinations have yet to be used.

	Up to 1974 (Codes used from 1903 to 1974 unless otherwise stated)	Last "Yearless" Mark	From 1974 onwards (Codes used from 1974 to 2001 or 1974 onwards for Northern Ireland codes)
A	1903-65 London CC 1965-74 Greater London	A 9999	
AA	Hampshire CC+	264 PAA	1974-80 Salisbury 1980-01 Bournemouth
AB	Worcestershire CC	7 NAB	Worcester
AC	Warwickshire CC	9999 AC 999 LAC	1974-96 Coventry 1996-01 Birmingham/ Northampton/Worcester
AD	Gloucestershire CC	9999 AD 999 BAD	1974-97 Gloucester 1997-01 Bristol/Worcester
AE	Bristol CBC	999 YAE	Bristol
AF	Cornwall CC	948 XAF	Truro
AG	1924-74 Ayr CC	YAG 999	1974-97 Hull 1997-01 Beverley@
AH	Norfolk CC	9999 AH 999 EAH	Norwich
AI	1903-86 Meath CC	9999 AI	
AJ	Yorkshire – North Riding CC	999 HAJ	1974-00 Middlesbrough 2000-01 Stockton@
AK	Bradford CBC	YAK 999	Sheffield
AL	Nottinghamshire CC	999 YAL	Nottingham
AM	Wiltshire CC	364 FAM	1974-97 Swindon 1997-01 Bristol
AN	1903-65 West Ham CBC 1965-74 Greater London	459 EAN	Reading
AO	Cumberland CC	184 NAO	Carlisle
AP	East Sussex CC	9975 AP	Brighton

AR	Hertfordshire CC	9999 AR 2 XAR	Chelmsford
AS*	Nairn CC	AS 4148	Inverness
AT	Hull CBC	999 HAT	1974-96 Hull 1996-01 Beverley@
AU	Nottingham CBC	999 UAU	Nottingham
AV	1924-74 Aberdeen CC	YAV 999	Peterborough
AW	Shropshire CC#	YAW 999 9999 AW	Shrewsbury
AX	Monmouth CC	253 KAX	Cardiff
AY	Leicestershire CC	865 FAY	1974-96 Leicester 1996-01 Birmingham/Nottingham/ Peterborough
AZ	1927-74 Belfast CBC	9999 AZ AAZ 9999	Belfast
B	Lancashire CC	B 9999	
BA	Salford CBC	YBA 999	Manchester
BB	Newcastle upon Tyne CBC	4067 BB 816 XBB	Newcastle upon Tyne
BC	Leicester CBC	400 JBC	1974-96 Leicester 1996-01 Birmingham/Nottingham/ Peterborough
BD	Northamptonshire CC	999 GBD	Northampton
BE	Lincolnshire – Lindsay CC	999 HBE	1974-80 Grimsby 1980-01 Lincoln
BF*	1903-20 Dorset CC 1960-74 Staffordshire CC	999 YBF	1974-96 Stoke 1996-01 Birmingham/Shrewsbury
BG	1928-74 Birkenhead CBC 1974 Wirral BC	RBG 999	1974-96 Liverpool 1996-01 AFRL issues only
BH	Buckinghamshire CC	999 YBH 9999 BH	Luton
BI	1903-86 Monaghan CC	6540 BI	
BJ	1903-71 East Suffolk 1971-74 Ipswich and East Suffolk	771 WBJ	Ipswich
BK	Portsmouth CBC	361 EBK	Portsmouth
BL	1903-73 Berkshire CC 1973-74 Berkshire CC and Reading CBC	999 GBL	Reading
BM	Bedfordshire CC	999 RBM	Luton
BN	Bolton CBC	YBN 999	1974-81 Bolton 1981-01 Manchester
BO	1903-73 Cardiff CBC 1973-74 Cardiff CBC and Glamorgan CC	999 FBO	Cardiff
BP	West Sussex CC	9999 BP 999 PBP	Portsmouth
BR	Sunderland CBC	YBR 517	1974-81 Durham 1981-01 Newcastle upon Tyne
BS*	Orkney CC	BS 7938	1974-80 Kirkwall 1980-01 Inverness
BT	Yorkshire – East Riding CC	9999 BT 999 CBT	1974-80 York 1980-01 Leeds

BU	Oldham CBC	362 KBU	Manchester
BV	1928-74 Blackburn CBC	SBV 999	Preston
BW	1903-72 Oxfordshire CC 1972-74 Oxford CBC and Oxfordshire CC	YBW 999	Oxford
BX	Carmarthen CC	999 FBX	1974-96 Haverfordwest 1996-01 Swansea
BY	1903-65 Croydon CBC 1965-74 Greater London	999 EBY	1974-91 London North West 1991-92 Ruislip 1992-01 Stanmore@
BZ	Down CC	9999 BZ YBZ 9999	1974-14 Downpatrick
C	Yorkshire – West Riding CBC	C 9999	
CA	Denbigh CC	916 BCA	Chester
CB	Blackburn CBC	SCB 999	1974-81 Bolton 1981-01 Manchester
CC	Caernarvon CC	OJC 685	Bangor
CD	Brighton CBC	9999 CD 998 FCD	Brighton
CE	1903-65 Cambridgeshire CC 1965-74 Cambridgeshire & Isle of Ely CC	114 FCE	1976-80 Cambridge 1980-01 – Peterborough
CF	West Suffolk CC	342 ACF	Reading
CG	1930-74 Hampshire CC+	999 NCG	1974-80 Salisbury 1980-01 Bournemouth
CH	Derby CBC	981 FCH	Nottingham
CI	1903-21 Queens County 1921-86 Laoighis CC &	7342 CI	
CJ	Hereford CC	999 ECJ	1974-81 Hereford 1981-97 Gloucester 1987-01 Bristol & Worcester
CK	Preston CBC	VCK 574	Preston
CL	Norwich CBC	YCL 999	Norwich
CM	Birkenhead CBC 1974 Wirral BC	SCM 991	1974-96 Liverpool 1996-01 Not used
CN	Gateshead CBC	SCN 210	Newcastle upon Tyne
CO	Plymouth CBC	YCO 999	1974-80 Plymouth 1980-01 Exeter (not used)
CP	Halifax CBC	UCP 171	1974-94 Huddersfield 1994-01 Leeds
CR	Southampton CBC	999 HCR	Portsmouth
CS	Ayr CC	YCS 999	1974-81 Ayr 1981-01 Glasgow
CT	Lincolnshire – Kesteven CC	YCT 999	1974-81 Boston 1981-01 Lincoln
CU	South Shields CBC	NCU 280	Newcastle upon Tyne
CV	1928-74 Cornwall CC	999 WCV	Truro
CW	Burnley CBC	RCW 725	Preston
CX	Huddersfield CBC	YCX 999 1164 CX	1974-94 Huddersfield 1994-01 Leeds
CY	Swansea CBC %	999 JCY	Swansea
CZ	Belfast CBC	9999 CZ YCZ 9999	Belfast

D	Kent CC	6801 D	
DA	Wolverhampton CBC	9999 DA 572 GDA	Birmingham
DB	Stockport CBC	YDB 999	Manchester
DC	1903-68 Middlesbrough CBC 1968-74 Teeside CBC	SDC 999	1974-00 Middlesbrough 2000-01 Stockton@
DD	Gloucestershire CC	9999 DD 641 BDD	1974-97 Gloucester 1997-01 Bristol/Worcester
DE	Pembroke CC	585 YDE	1974-96 Haverfordwest 1996-01 Swansea
DF	1903-20 Northampton CBC 1924-74 Gloucestershire CC	999 ADF 9999 DF	1974-97 Gloucester 1997-01 Bristol/Worcester
DG	1928-74 Gloucestershire CC	999 ADG 5405 DG	1974-97 Gloucester 1997-01 Bristol/Worcester
DH	Walsall CBC	6073 DH 76 XDH	1974-93 Dudley 1993-01 Birmingham
DI	1903-86 Roscommon CC	9999 DI 292 BDI	
DJ	St Helens CBC	XDJ 331	1974-81 Warrington 1981-96 Liverpool 1996-01 Preston
DK	Rochdale CBC	7821 DK 309 ADK	1974-81 Bolton 1981-01 Manchester
DL	Isle of Wight CC	862 CDL	1974-81 Newport 1981-01 Portsmouth
DM	Flint CC	89 JDM	Chester
DN	York CBC	9999 DN 999 BDN	1974-80 York 1980-01 Leeds
DO	Lincolnshire – Holland CC	YDO 999	1974-81 Boston 1981-01 Lincoln
DP	1903-73 Reading CBC 1973-74 Berkshire CC and Reading CBC	9999 DP	Reading
DR	1903-14 Devonport CBC 1914-74 Plymouth CBC	YDR 999	1974-80 Plymouth 1980-01 Exeter (not used)
DS*	Peebles CC	DS 9999	Glasgow
DT	1927-74 Doncaster CBC	9999 DT, 471 RDT	Sheffield
DU	Coventry CBC	999 CDU 2337 DU	1974-96 Coventry 1996-01 Birmingham/ Northampton/Worcester
DV	1928-74 Devon CC	999 TDV	Exeter
DW	Newport CBC	5453 DW 235 BDW	Cardiff
DX	1903-71 Ipswich CBC 1971-74 Ipswich CBC and East Suffolk CC	VDX 719	Ipswich
DY	Hastings CBC	VDY 601	1974-80 Hastings 1980-01 Brighton
DZ	Antrim CC	9999 DZ YDZ 9999	Ballymena
E	Staffordshire CC	9999 E	
EA	West Bromwich CBC	331 UEA	1974-93 Dudley 1993-01 Birmingham

EB	1903-65 Isle of Ely CC 1965-74 Cambridgeshire and Isle of Ely CC	REB 999	1974-80 Cambridge 1980-01 Peterborough
EC	Westmorland CC	MEC 999	1974-81 Kendal 1981-01 Preston
ED	Warrington CBC	8814 ED 999 AED	1974-81 Warrington 1981-96 Liverpool 1996-01 Preston
EE	Grimsby CBC	YEE 999	1974-80 Grimsby 1980-01 Lincoln
EF	1903-67 West Hartlepool CBC 1967-74 Hartlepool CBC	REF 640	1974-00 Middlesbrough 2000-01 Stockton@
EG	1930-65 Soke of Peterborough CC 1965-74 Huntingdon and Peterborough CC	YEG 460	Peterborough
EH	1903-10 Hanley CBC 1910-74 Stoke-on-Trent CBC	999 YEH 9215 EH	1974-96 Stoke-on-Trent 1996-01 Birmingham/Shrewsbury
EI	1903-86 Sligo CC	835 AEI	
EJ	Cardigan CC	SEJ 847	1974-81 Aberystwyth 1981-83 Bangor 1983-96 Haverfordwest 1996-01 Swansea
EK	Wigan CBC	LEK 999	1974-81 Warrington 1981-96 Liverpool 1996-01 Preston
EL	Bournemouth CBC	9999 EL 492 DEL	Bournemouth
EM	Bootle CBC	DEM 11	1974-96 Liverpool 1996-01 AFRL issues only
EN	Bury CBC	VEN 294	1974-81 Bolton 1981-01 Manchester
EO	Barrow-in-Furness CBC	MEO 365	1974-81 Barrow-in-Furness 1981-01 Preston
EP	Montgomery CC	TEP 898	Swansea
ER	1921-65 Cambridgeshire CC 1965-74 Cambridgeshire and Isle of Ely CC	998 EER	1974-80 Cambridge 1980-01 Peterborough
ES	Perth CC	VES 999	Dundee
ET	Rotherham CBC	8794 ET 530 BET	Sheffield
EU	Brecon CC	PEU 700	Bristol
EV	1928-74 Essex CC	9999 EV 999 YEV	Chelmsford
EW	1903-65 Huntingdon CC 1965-74 Huntingdon and Peterborough CC	874 MEW	Peterborough
EX	Great Yarmouth CBC	KEX 999	Norwich
EY	Anglesey CC	PEY 436	Bangor
EZ	Belfast CBC	9999 EZ YEZ 9999	Belfast
F	Essex CC	9999 F	
FA	Burton-on-Trent CBC	UFA 763	1974-96 Stoke-on-Trent 1996-01 Birmingham/Shrewsbury

FB	Bath CBC	PFB 157	Bristol
FC	1903-72 Oxford CBC 1972-74 Oxford CBC and Oxfordshire CC	999 VFC	Oxford
FD	Dudley CBC	9999 FD 901 EFD	1974-93 Dudley 1993-01 Birmingham
FE	Lincoln CBC	XVL 387	Lincoln
FF*	Merioneth CC	HFF 988	1974-81 Aberystwyth 1981-01 Bangor
FG	1923-74 Fife CC	700 FG 8000 FG	Brighton
FH	Gloucester CBC	9999 FH 286 FFH	1974-97 Gloucester 1997-01 Bristol/Worcester
FI	1903-86 Tipperary – North Riding CC	418 JFI	
FJ	Exeter CBC	248 JFJ	Exeter
FK	Worcester CBC	999 JFK 5114 FK	1974-93 Dudley 1993-01 Birmingham
FL	1903-65 Soke of Peterborough CC 1965-74 Huntingdon and Peterborough CC	UFL 999	Peterborough
FM	Chester CBC	999 YFM 8635 FM	Chester
FN	Canterbury CBC	9999 FN	1974-81 Canterbury 1981-01 Maidstone
FO*	Radnor CC	EFO 573	1974-81 Hereford 1981-97 Gloucester 1987-01 Bristol & Worcester
FP	Rutland CC	DFP 601	1974-96 Leicester 1996-01 Birmingham/Nottingham/Peterborough
FR	1904-74 Blackpool CBC	884 JFR	Preston
FS	1928-74 Edinburgh BC	2556 FS	Edinburgh
FT	1904-74 Tynemouth CBC	KFT 500	Newcastle upon Tyne
FU	1922-74 Lincolnshire – Lindsey CC	998 HFU	1974-81 Grimsby 1981-01 Lincoln
FV	1928-74 Blackpool CBC	YFV 999	Preston
FW	1929-74 Lincolnshire – Lindsey CC	272 HFW	1974-81 Grimsby 1981-01 Lincoln
FX	1904-74 Dorset CBC	WFX 527	Bournemouth
FY	1904-74 Southport CBC	40 AFY	1974-96 Liverpool 1996-01 Not used
FZ	1937-74 Belfast CBC	9999 FZ YFZ 9999	Belfast
G	Glasgow BC	G 9999	
GA	1917-74 Glasgow BC	999 KGA	Glasgow
GB	1921-74 Glasgow BC	999 KGB	ditto
GC	1928-65 London CC 1965-74 Greater London	121 KGC	1974-91 London South West 1991-97 Croydon 1997-01 Wimbledon@
GD	1924-74 Glasgow BC	999 KGD	Glasgow
GE	1926-74 Glasgow BC	999 KGE	ditto

GF	1928-65 London CC 1965-74 Greater London	986 JGF	1974-91 London South West 1991-97 Croydon 1997-01 Wimbledon@
GG	1928-74 Glasgow BC	999 JGG	Glasgow
GH	1928-65 London CC 1965-74 Greater London	999 JGH	1974-91 London South West 1991-97 Croydon 1997-01 Wimbledon@
GI	1981-86 Tipperary – South Riding CC	CGI 871	GI **** combinations not issued
GJ	1928-65 London CC 1965-74 Greater London	999 JGJ	1974-91 London South West 1991-97 Croydon 1997-01 Wimbledon@
GK	ditto	999 JGK	ditto
GL	1930-74 Bath CBC	PGL 1	Truro
GM	1921-74 Motherwell and Wishaw BC	GGM 1	Reading
GN	1928-65 London CC 1965-74 Greater London	999 JGN	1974-91 London South West 1991-97 Croydon 1997-01 Wimbledon@
GO	ditto	999 JGO	ditto
GP	ditto	999 JGP	ditto
GR	1930-74 Sunderland CBC	XGR 999	1974-81 Durham 1981-01 Newcastle upon Tyne
GS	1924-74 Perth CC	VGS 975	Luton
GT	1928-65 London CC 1965-74 Greater London	787 JGT	1974-91 London South West 1991-97 Croydon 1997-01 Wimbledon@
GU	ditto	999 LGU	ditto
GV	1928-74 West Suffolk CC	YGV 999	Ipswich
GW	1928-65 London CC 1965-74 Greater London	999 JGW	1974-91 London South East 1991-93 Sidcup 1993-97 Wimbledon@ 1997-01 Sidcup@
GX	ditto	999 JGX	ditto
GY	ditto	846 JGY	ditto
GZ	1942-74 Belfast CBC	9999 GZ In use	Belfast
H	Middlesex CC	9999 H	
HA	1907-66 Smethwick CBC 1966-74 Warley CBC	9720 HA 650 SHA 39 THA	1974-93 Dudley 1993-01 Birmingham
HB	1908-74 Merthyr Tydfil CBC	EHB 439	Cardiff
HC	1910-74 Eastbourne CBC	MHC 999	1974-80 Hastings 1980-01 Brighton
HD	1912-74 Dewsbury CBC	LHD 816	1974-94 Huddersfield 1994-01 Leeds
HE	1912-74 Barnsley CBC	6923 HE	Sheffield
HF	1912-74 Wallasey CBC 1974 Wirral MC	OHF 925	1974-96 Liverpool 1996-01 AFRL issues only
HG	1928-74 Burnley CBC	PHG 725	Preston
HH	1914-74 Carlisle CBC	YHH 873	Carlisle
HI	1903-86 Tipperary – South Riding CC	ZHI 999	

HJ	1914-74 Southend-on-Sea CBC	9999 HJ 783 BHJ	Chelmsford
HK	1914-74 Essex CC	9999 HK 999 YHK	Chelmsford
HL	1915-74 Wakefield CBC	4237 HL	Sheffield
HM	1915-65 East Ham CBC 1965-74 Greater London	YHM 999	1974-97 London Central 1997-01 Wimbledon
HN	1915-74 Darlington CBC	9999 HN 343 YHN	1974-00 Middlesbrough 2000-01 Stockton@
HO	1916-74 Hampshire CC	999 NHO	1974-80 Salisbury 1980-01 Bournemouth
HP	1919-74 Coventry CBC	9999 HP 999 CHP	1974-96 Coventry 1996-01 Birmingham/ Northampton/Worcester
HR	1919-74 Wiltshire CC	999 HER	1974-97 Swindon 1997-01 Bristol
HS	Renfrew CC	YHS 999	Glasgow
HT	1920-74 Bristol CBC	211 YHT	Bristol
HU	1921-74 Bristol CBC	999 XHU	ditto
HV	1928-65 East Ham CBC 1965-74 Greater London	YHV 363	1974-97 London Central 1997-01 Wimbledon
HW	1928-74 Bristol CBC	999 XHW	Bristol
HX	1928-65 Middlesex CC 1965-74 Greater London	999 YHX 9999 HX	1974-97 London Central 1997-01 Wimbledon
HY	1928-74 Bristol CBC	999 XHY	Bristol
HZ	1943-74 Tyrone CC	9999 HZ In use	Omagh
IA	Antrim CC	9999 IA 999 YIA	Ballymena
IB	Armagh CC	9999 IB YIB 9999	Armagh
IC	1903-86 Carlow CC	YIC 994	
ID	1903-86 Cavan CC	9999 ID 906 IID	
IE	1903-86 Clare CC	9999 IE 906 XIE	
IF	Cork CC 1974-86 Cork CC & Cork CBC	9999 IF 999 ZIF	
IG		In use	From 2005 onwards – Enniskillen
IH	1903-86 Donegal	9999 IH	
IJ	Down	9999 IJ YIJ 999	Downpatrick
IK	1903-52 Dublin CC 1952-86 Dublin CC & Dublin CBC	9999 IK 999 ZIK	
IL	1958-74 Fermanagh CC	9999 IL YIL 9999	Enniskillen
IM	1903-86 Galway CC	9999 IM 999 ZIM	
IN	1903-86 Kerry CC	9999 IN 999 ZIN	
IO	1903-86 Kildare CC	ZIO 999	
IP	1903-86 Kilkenny CC	9999 IP	

		235 UIP	
IR	1903-21 Kings County 1921-86 Offaly CC &	7834 IR	
IS	1981-86 Mayo CC	HIS 990	IS **** combinations not issued
IT	1903-86 Leitrim CC	KIT 780	
IU	1903-86 Limerick CC	9999 IU 999 ZIU	
IV	1981-86 Limerick CC	OIV 520	IV **** combinations not issued
IW	Londonderry CC	9999 IW YIW 9999	Coleraine
IX	1903-86 Longford CC	PIX 710	
IY	1903-86 Louth CC	ZIY 999	
IZ	1903-86 Mayo CC	9999 IZ 999 ZIZ	
J	Durham CC	J 9999	
JA	1928-74 Stockport CBC	YJA 999	Manchester
JB	1928-74 Berkshire CC 1973-74 Berkshire CC and Reading CBC	999 GJB	Reading
JC	1928-74 Caernarvon CC	OJC 674	Bangor
JD	1928-65 West Ham CBC 1964-74 Greater London	459 EAN	1974-97 London Central 1997-01 Wimbledon
JE	1928-63 Isle of Ely CC 1963-74 Cambridgeshire and Isle of Ely CC	RJE 6	1974-80 Cambridge 1980-01 Peterborough
JF	1928-74 Leicester CBC		1974-96 Leicester 1996-01 Birmingham/Nottingham/ Peterborough
JG	1928-74 Canterbury CBC	1551 JG	1974-81 Canterbury 1981-01 Maidstone
JH	1928-74 Hertfordshire CC	9999 JH 999 WJH	Reading
JI	Tyrone CC	9999 JI YJI 9999	Omagh
JJ	1932-65 London CC 1965-74 Greater London	999 HJJ	1974-81 Canterbury 1981-01 Maidstone
JK	1928-74 Eastbourne CBC	MJK 444	1974-80 Hastings 1980-01 Brighton
JL	1928-74 Lincolnshire – Holland CC	YJL 999	1974-81 Boston 1981-01 Lincoln
JM	1928-74 Westmorland CC	MJM 498	Reading
JN	1928-74 Southend-on-Sea CBC	999 AJN 5507 JN	Chelmsford
JO	1928-72 Oxford CBC 1972-74 Oxford CBC and Oxfordshire CC	435 VJO	Oxford
JP	1928-74 Wigan CBC	LJP 628	1974-81 Warrington 1981-96 Liverpool 1996-01 Preston
JR	1928-74 Northumberland CC	YJR 999	Newcastle upon Tyne
JS	Ross and Cromarty CC	NJS 426	1974-80 Stornoway 1980-01 Inverness
JT	Dorset CC	VJT 999	Bournemouth

JU	1928-74 Leicestershire CC	999 EJU	1974-96 Leicester 1996-01 Birmingham/Nottingham/ Peterborough
JV	1928-74 Grimsby CBC	YJV 999	1974-80 Grimsby 1980-01 Lincoln
JW	1928-74 Wolverhampton CBC	9999 JW 999 FJW	Bournemouth
JX	1928-74 Halifax CBC	TJX 999	1974-94 Huddersfield 1994-01 Leeds
JY	1928-74 Plymouth CBC	YJY 999	1974-80 Plymouth 1980-01 Exeter (not used)
JZ	1946-74 Down CC	9999 JZ YJZ 9999	Downpatrick
K	Liverpool CBC	9999 K	
KA	1922-74 Liverpool CBC	9999 KA 999 JKA	1974-96 Liverpool 1996-01 AFRL issues only
KB	1914-74 Liverpool CBC	9999 KB 999 JKB	ditto
KC	1920-74 Liverpool CBC	9999 KC 545 JKC	ditto
KD	1926-74 Liverpool CBC	9999 KD 999 HKD	ditto
KE	1920-74 Kent CC	999 YKE	Maidstone
KF	1928-74 Liverpool CBC	9999 KF 999 HKF	1974-96 Liverpool 1996-01 AFRL issues only
KG	1928-73 Cardiff CBC 1973-74 Cardiff CBC and Glamorgan CC	999 FKG	Cardiff
KH	1923-74 Hull CBC	9999 KH 999 HKH	1974-96 Hull 1996-01 Beverley@
KI	1903-86 Waterford CC	9999 KI 586 AKI	
KJ	1930-74 Kent CC	999 YKJ	Maidstone
KK	1921-74 Kent CC	999 YKK	ditto
KL	1923-74 Kent CC	999 YKL	ditto
KM	1924-74 Kent CC	9999 KM 999 YKM	ditto
KN	1917-74 Kent CC	9999 KN 999 YKN	ditto
KO	1924-74 Kent CC	9999 KO 999 YKO	ditto
KP	1926-74 Kent CC	9999 KP 999 YKP	ditto
KR	1923-74 Kent CC	9999 KR 999 YKR	ditto
KS	Roxburgh CC	SKS 297	1974-75 St Boswells 1975-80 Selkirk@ 1980-01 Edinburgh
KT	1913-74 Kent CC	999 YKT	1974-81 Canterbury 1981-01 Maidstone
KU	1921-74 Bradford CBC	YKU 999	Sheffield
KV	1928-74 Coventry CBC	9998 KV 999 AKV	1974-96 Coventry 1996-01 Birmingham/ Northampton/Worcester

KW	1924-74 Bradford CBC	9999 KW	Sheffield
KX	1926-74 Buckinghamshire CC	999 YKX 9990 KX	Luton
KY	1928-74 Bradford CBC	9999 KY	Sheffield
KZ	Antrim CC	9999 KZ YKZ 9999	Ballymena
L	1903-73 Glamorgan CC 1973-74 Cardiff CBC and Glamorgan CC	L 9999	
LA	1910-65 London CC 1965-74 Greater London	982 JLA	1976-91 London North West 1991-92 Ruislip 1992-01 Stanmore@
LB	1907-65 London CC 1965-74 Greater London	666 JLB	ditto
LC	1905-65 London CC 1965-74 Greater London	969 JLC	ditto
LD	1909-65 London CC 1965-74 Greater London	999 HLD	ditto
LE	1911-65 London CC 1965-74 Greater London	999 HLE	ditto
LF	1912-65 London CC 1965-74 Greater London	999 HLF	ditto
LG	1928-74 Cheshire CC	999 YLG 9999 LG	Chester
LH	1912-65 London CC 1965-74 Greater London	999 HLH	1976-91 London North West 1991-92 Ruislip 1992-01 Stanmore@
LI	Westmeath CC	9999 LI 869 GLI	
LJ	1928-74 Bournemouth CBC	9999 LJ 999 CLJ	Bournemouth
LK	1913-65 London CC 1965-74 Greater London	999 HLK	1976-91 London North West 1991-92 Ruislip 1992-01 Stanmore@
LL	1914-65 London CC 1965-74 Greater London	999 HLL	ditto
LM	1914-65 London CC 1965-74 Greater London	999 HLM	ditto
LN	1906-65 London CC 1965-74 Greater London	999 HLN	ditto
LO	1914-65 London CC 1965-74 Greater London	999 HLO	ditto
LP	1915-65 London CC 1965-74 Greater London	999 HLP	ditto
LR	1916-65 London CC 1965-74 Greater London	999 HLR	ditto
LS	Selkirk CC	LS 9701	1974-81 Stirling 1981-01 Edinburgh
LT	1917-65 London CC 1965-74 Greater London	999 HLT	1976-91 London North West 1991-92 Ruislip 1992-01 Stanmore@
LU	1918-65 London CC 1965-74 Greater London	999 HLU	Ditto
LV	1930-74 Liverpool	9999 LV	1974-96 Liverpool

		999 HLV	1996-01 AFRL issues only
LW	1919-65 London CC 1965-74 Greater London	999 HLW	1976-91 London North West 1991-92 Ruislip 1992-01 Stanmore@
LX	1919-65 London CC 1965-74 Greater London	999 HLX	ditto
LY	1919-65 London CC 1965-74 Greater London	999 HLY	ditto
LZ	1946-74 Armagh CC	9999 LZ YLZ 9999	Armagh
M	Cheshire CC	M 9999	
MA	1918-74 Cheshire CC	999 YMA	Chester
MB	1921-74 Cheshire CC	999 YMB	ditto
MC	1916-65 Middlesex CC 1965-74 Greater London	999 YMC 9999 MC	1974-91 London North West 1991-96 Ilford 1996-01 Chelmsford
MD	1919-65 Middlesex CC 1965-74 Greater London	999 YMD 9999 MD	ditto
ME	1920-65 Middlesex CC 1965-74 Greater London	999 YME 9999 ME	ditto
MF	1922-65 Middlesex CC 1965-74 Greater London	999 YMF 9999 MF	ditto
MG	1928-65 Middlesex CC 1965-74 Greater London	999 YMG 9999 MG	ditto
MH	1923-65 Middlesex CC 1965-74 Greater London	999 YMH 9999 MH	ditto
MI	1903-86 Wexford CC	9999 MI	ditto
MJ	1928-74 Bedfordshire CC	999 PMJ	Luton
MK	1924-65 Middlesex CC 1965-74 Greater London	999 YMK 9999 MK	1974-91 London North West 1991-96 Ilford 1996-01 Chelmsford
ML	1926-65 Middlesex CC 1965-74 Greater London	999 YML 9999 ML	ditto
MM	1924-65 Middlesex CC 1965-74 Greater London	999 YMM 9999 MM	ditto
MN	Not used to avoid possible confusion with Isle of Man numbers		
MO	1921-73 Berkshire CC 1973-74 Berkshire CC and Reading CBC	402 GMO	Reading
MP	1926-65 Middlesex CC 1965-74 Greater London	999 YMP 9999 MP	1974-91 London North West 1991-96 Ilford 1996-01 Chelmsford
MR	1921-74 Wiltshire CC	999 EMR	1974-97 Swindon 1997-01 Bristol
MS	Stirling CC	YMS 362	1974-81 Stirling 1981-01 Edinburgh
MT	1926-65 Middlesex CC 1965-74 Greater London	999 YMT 9999 MT	1974-91 London North West 1991-96 Ilford 1996-01 Chelmsford
MU	1928-65 Middlesex CC 1965-74 Greater London	999 YMU 9999 MU	Ditto
MV	1928-65 Middlesex CC 1965-74 Greater London	999 UMV 9999 MV	1974-91 London South East 1991-93 Sidcup 1993-97 Wimbledon@

			1997-01 Sidcup@
MW	1926-74 Wiltshire CC	9999 MW 999 EMW	1974-97 Swindon 1997-01 Bristol
MX	1912-65 Middlesex CC 1965-74 Greater London	999 YMX 9999 MX	ditto
MY	1926-65 Middlesex CC 1965-74 Greater London	999 YMY 9999 MY	ditto
MZ	1947-74 Belfast CBC	9999 MZ	Belfast
N	Manchester	9999 N	
NA	1913-74 Manchester CBC	9999 NA	Manchester
NB	1919-74 Manchester CBC	9999 NB	ditto
NC	1920-74 Manchester CBC	9999 NC	ditto
ND	1921-74 Manchester CBC	9999 ND	ditto
NE	1923-74 Manchester CBC	9999 NE	ditto
NF	1924-74 Manchester CBC	9999 NF	ditto
NG	1928-74 Norfolk CC	9999 NG 999 ENG	Norwich
NH	1905-74 Northampton CBC	TNH 999	Northampton
NI	1903-86 Wicklow CC	426 TNI	
NJ	1930-74 East Sussex CC	YNJ 999	Brighton
NK	1920-74 Hertfordshire CC	9999 WK 522 WNK	Luton
NL	1920-74 Northumberland CC	YNL 999	Newcastle upon Tyne
NM	1920-74 Bedfordshire CC	205 RNM	Luton
NN	Nottingham CC	999 YNN	Nottingham
NO	1920-74 Essex CC	9999 NO 999 YNO	Chelmsford
NP	1921-74 Worcestershire CC	999 MNP	Worcester
NR	1921-74 Leicestershire CC	999 ENR	1974-96 Leicester 1996-01 Birmingham/Nottingham/ Peterborough
NS	Sutherland CC	NS 5756	Glasgow
NT	1921-74 Shropshire CC#	5130 NT	Shrewsbury
NU	1921-74 Derbyshire CC	999 YNU 9999 NU	Nottingham
NV	1928-74 Northamptonshire CC	999 GNV	Northampton
NW	1921-74 Leeds CBC	9999 NW 999 LNW	Leeds
NX	1921-74 Warwickshire CC	9999 NX 999 LNX	1974-93 Dudley 1993-01 Birmingham
NY	1921-73 Glamorgan CC 1973-74 Cardiff CBC and Glamorgan CC	YNY 999	Cardiff
NZ	1948-74 Londonderry CC	9999 NZ In use	Coleraine
O	Birmingham CBC	O 9999	
OA	1912-74 Birmingham CBC	999 NOA	Birmingham
OB	1915-74 Birmingham CBC	999 NOB	ditto
OC	1922-74 Birmingham CBC	999 NOC	ditto
OD	1930-74 Devon CC	999 TOD	Exeter
OE	1919-74 Birmingham CBC	999 NOE	Birmingham
OF	1928-74 Birmingham CBC	999 NOF	ditto
OG	1928-74 Birmingham CBC	896 NOG	ditto

OH	1920-74 Birmingham CBC	999 NOH	ditto
OI	Belfast	9999 OI AOI 9999	Belfast
OJ	1930-74 Birmingham CBC	999 NOJ	Birmingham
OK	1921-74 Birmingham CBC	999 NOK	ditto
OL	1923-74 Birmingham CBC	26 NOL	ditto
OM	1923-74 Birmingham CBC	999 MOM	ditto
ON	1924-74 Birmingham CBC	999 MON	ditto
OO	1961-74 Essex CC	9999 OO 999 YOO	Chelmsford
OP	1924-74 Birmingham CBC	999 MOP	Birmingham
OR	1921-74 Hampshire CC+	999 NOR	Portsmouth
OS	Wigtown CC	HOS 753	1974-81 Stranraer 1981-01 Glasgow
OT	1924-74 Hampshire CC+	999 NOT	Portsmouth
OU	1928-74 Hampshire CC+	999 NOU	Bristol
OV	1928-74 Birmingham CBC	999 MOV	Birmingham
OW	1928-74 Southampton CBC	1 HOW	Portsmouth
OX	1926-74 Birmingham CBC	999 MOX	Birmingham
OY	1928-65 Croydon CBC 1965-74 Greater London	999 EOY	1976-91 London North West 1991-92 Ruislip 1992-01 Stanmore@
OZ	1950-74 Belfast CBC	9999 OZ	Belfast
P	Surrey CC	P 9999	
PA	1913-74 Surrey CC	999 YPA	1974-97 Guildford 1997-01 Portsmouth/Reading/ Wimbledon
PB	1919-74 Surrey CC	999 YPB	ditto
PC	1921-74 Surrey CC	999 YPC	ditto
PD	1922-74 Surrey CC	999 YPD	ditto
PE	1923-74 Surrey CC	999 YPE 9494 PE	ditto
PF	1924-74 Surrey CC	999 YPF 9999 PF	ditto
PG	1928-74 Surrey CC	999 YPG 9999 PG	ditto
PH	1924-74 Surrey CC	999 YPH 9999 PH	ditto
PI	Cork CBC 1974-86 Cork CC & Cork CBC	9999 PI 999 ZPI	
PJ	1930-74 Surrey CC	999 YPJ 9999 PJ	1974-97 Guildford 1997-01 Portsmouth/Reading/ Wimbledon
PK	1926-74 Surrey CC	999 YPK 9999 PK	ditto
PL	1928-74 Surrey CC	999 YPL 9999 PL	ditto
PM	1922-74 East Sussex CC	YPM 999	ditto
PN	1926-74 East Sussex CC	YPN 999	Brighton
PO	1926-74 West Sussex CC	9999 PO 851 PPO	Portsmouth
PP	1922-74 Buckinghamshire CC	999 YPP 7846 PP	Luton

PR	1922-74 Dorset CC	VPR 999	Bournemouth
PS	Zetland	PS 4094	1974-80 Lerwick 1980-01 Aberdeen
PT	1922-74 Durham CC	9999 PT 438 NPT	1974-81 Durham 1981-01 Newcastle upon Tyne
PU	1922-74 Essex CC	999 YPU 9999 PU	Chelmsford
PV	1928-71 Ipswich CBC 1971-74 Ipswich CBC and East Suffolk CC	UPV 999	Ipswich
PW	1922-74 Norfolk CC	9999 PW 999 EPW	Norfolk
PX	1922-74 West Sussex CC	9999 PX 999 NPX	Portsmouth
PY	1922-74 Yorkshire – North Riding CC	439 HPY	1974-00 Middlesbrough 2000-01 Stockton@
PZ	1952-74 Belfast CBC	9999 PZ	Belfast
QA-QY	Used for temporary imports to 2001. See chapter 10.		
R	Derbyshire CC	9999 R	
RA	1924-74 Derbyshire CC	999 YRA 4749 RA	Nottingham
RB	1928-74 Derbyshire CC	999 YRB	ditto
RC	1928-74 Derby CBC	999 ERC	ditto
RD	1926-73 Reading CBC 1973-74 Berkshire CC and Reading CBC	2305 RD	Reading
RE	1923-74 Staffordshire CC	999 YRE 9999 RF	1974-96 Stoke-on-Trent 1996-01 Birmingham/Shrewsbury
RF	1924-74 Staffordshire CC	999 YRF 9999 RF	ditto
RG	1926-74 Aberdeen BC	WRG 999	Newcastle upon Tyne
RH	1928-74 Hull CBC	9999 RH 933 HRH	1974-96 Hull 1996-01 Beverley@
RI	1903-52 Dublin CBC 1952-86 Dublin CC & Dublin CBC	9999 RI 999 YRI	
RJ	1930-74 Salford CBC	YRJ 999	Manchester
RK	1922-65 Croydon CBC 1965-74 Greater London	9999 RK 999 DRK	1976-91 London North West 1991-92 Ruislip 1992-01 Stanmore@
RL	1923-74 Cornwall CC	999 WRL	Truro
RM	1923-74 Cumberland CC	999 MRM	Carlisle
RN	1928-74 Preston CBC	URN 999	Preston
RO	1923-74 Hertfordshire CC	9999 RO 999 VRO	Luton
RP	1923-74 Northamptonshire CC	335 GRP	Northampton
RR	1923-74 Nottinghamshire CC	81 YRR	Nottingham
RS	Aberdeen BC	WRS 904	Aberdeen
RT	1923-71 East Suffolk CC 1971-74 Ipswich CBC and East Suffolk CC	999 VRT	Ipswich
RU	1923-74 Bournemouth CBC	9999 RU	Bournemouth

		999 CRU	
RV	1928-74 Portsmouth CBC	999 DRV	Portsmouth
RW	1923-74 Coventry CBC	9999 RW 999 CRW	1974-96 Coventry 1996-01 Birmingham/ Northampton/Worcester
RX	1926-73 Berkshire CC 1973-74 Berkshire CC and Reading CBC	999 FRX	Reading
RY	1923-74 Leicester CBC	999 HRY	1974-96 Leicester 1996-01 Birmingham/Nottingham/ Peterborough
RZ	1954-74 Antrim CC	9999 RZ In use	Ballymena
S	Edinburgh BC	S 9999	
SA	Aberdeen CC	YSA 999	Aberdeen
SB	Argyll CC	NSB 431	1974-80 Oban 1980-01 Glasgow
SC	1926-74 Edinburgh BC	9999 SC	Edinburgh
SD	Ayr CC	YSD 836	1974-81 Ayr 1981-01 Glasgow
SE	Banff CC	JSE 1	1974-81 Keith 1981-01 Aberdeen
SF	1923-74 Edinburgh BC	9999 SF	Edinburgh
SG	1919-74 Edinburgh BC	YSG 999	ditto
SH	Berwick CC	KSH 747	1974-75 St Boswells 1975-80 Selkirk@ 1980-01 Edinburgh
SI	1981-86 Dublin CC & CBC	ZSI 999 SI 9999	
SJ *	Bute CC	SJ 2877	1974-81 Ayr 1981-01 Glasgow
SK*	Caithness CC	ASK 999	1974-81 Wick 1981-01 Inverness
SL*	Clackmannan CC	SL 9736	Dundee
SM	Dumfries CC	9999 SM 831 FSM	1974-81 Dumfries 1981-81 Glasgow 1981-01 Carlisle
SN	Dunbarton CC	WSN 305	Dundee
SO	1903-1919 Elgin CC 1919-74 Moray CC&	NSO 65	Aberdeen
SP	Fife CC	9999 SP	Dundee
SR	1903-28 Forfar CC 1928-74 Angus&	8981 SR 607 BSR$	Ditto
SS	1903-21 Haddington CC 1921-74 East Lothian CC&	JSS 468	Aberdeen
ST	Inverness CC	YST 738	Inverness
SU*	Kincardine CC	BSU 777	Glasgow
SV*	Kinross CC	SV 3786	
SW	Kirkcudbright CC	GSW 580	1974-81 Dumfries 1981-81 Glasgow 1981-01 Carlisle
SX	1903-21 Linlithgow CC 1921-74 West Lothian CC &	KSX 544	Edinburgh

SY *	Midlothian CC	NSY 469	
SZ	1954-74 Down CC	9999 SZ In use	Downpatrick
T	Devon CC	T 9999	
TA	1920-74 Devon CC	352 UTA	Exeter
TB	1919-74 Lancashire CC	999 YTB	1974-81 Warrington 1981-96 Liverpool 1996-01 Preston
TC	1921-74 Lancashire CC	999 YTC	Bristol
TD	1923-74 Lancashire CC	999 YTD 9999 TD	1974-81 Bolton 1981-01 Manchester
TE	1924-74 Lancashire CC	999 YTE 9999 TE	ditto
TF	1928-74 Lancashire CC	999 YTF 9999 TF	Manchester
TG	1928-73 Glamorgan CC 1973-74 Cardiff CBC and Glamorgan CC	23 YTG	Cardiff
TH	1926-74 Carmarthen CC	999 ETH	Swansea
TI	1903-86 Limerick CBC	929 FTI	
TJ	1930-74 Lancashire CC	999 YTJ 9999 TJ	1974-96 Liverpool 1996-01 AFRL issues only
TK	1926-74 Dorset CC	VTK 999	1974-80 Plymouth 1980-01 Exeter (not used)
TL	1926-74 Lincolnshire – Kesteven CC	YTL 999	Lincoln
TM	1924-74 Bedfordshire CC	999 PTM	Luton
TN	1923-74 Newcastle upon Tyne CBC	999 WTN	Newcastle upon Tyne
TO	1923-74 Nottingham CBC	720 UTO	Nottingham
TP	1923-74 Portsmouth CBC	999 DTP	Portsmouth
TR	1923-74 Southampton CBC	999 HTR	Portsmouth
TS	Dundee BC	STS 480	Dundee
TT	1923-74 Devon CC	999 TTT	Exeter
TU	1924-74 Cheshire CC	999 YTU 7697 TU	Chester
TV	1928-74 Nottingham CBC	999 TTV	Nottingham
TW	1924-74 Essex CC	999 YTW 9999 TW	Chelmsford
TX	1924-73 Glamorgan CC 1973-74 Cardiff CBC and Glamorgan CC	999 XTX	Cardiff
TY	1924-74 Northumberland CC	YTY 999	Newcastle upon Tyne
TZ	1954-74 Belfast CBC	9999 TZ	Belfast
U	Leeds CBC	9999 U	
UA*	1923-74 Leeds CBC	9999 UA 999 LUA	Leeds
UB*	1928-74 Leeds CBC	9999 UB 999 LUB	ditto
UC*	1926-65 London CC 1965-74 Greater London	999 HUC	1974-97 London Central 1997-01 Wimbledon
UD*	1924-72 Oxfordshire CC	YUD 999	Oxford

	1972-74 Oxford CBC and Oxfordshire CC		
UE*	1924-74 Warwickshire CC	9999 UE 122 LUE	1974-93 Dudley 1993-01 Birmingham
UF*	1924-74 Brighton CBC	923 FUF	Brighton
UG*	1930-74 Leeds CBC	9999 UG 999 LUG	Leeds
UH*	1924-73 Cardiff CBC 1973-74 Cardiff CBC and Glamorgan CC	388 FUH	Cardiff
UI	Londonderry CBC	9999 UI In use	Londonderry
UJ*	1930-74 Shropshire CC	YUJ 999	Shrewsbury
UK*	1924-74 Wolverhampton CBC	9999 UK 999 EUK	Birmingham
UL*	1926-65 London CC 1965-74 Greater London	999 HUL	1974-97 London Central 1997-01 Wimbledon
UM*	1922-74 Leeds CBC	9999 UM 412 LUM	Leeds
UN*	1924-74 Denbighshire CC	9999 UN 999 AUN	1974-81 Barnstaple 1981-01 Exeter (not used)
UO*	1924-74 Devon CC	999 TUO	ditto
UP*	1924-74 Durham CC	9999 UP 751 MUP	1974-81 Durham 1981-01 Newcastle upon Tyne
UR*	1924-74 Hertfordshire CC	9999 UR 999 VUR	Luton
US*	1903-12 Govan BC 1912-74 Glasgow BC	999 JUS	Glasgow
UT*	1924-74 Leicestershire CC	999 EUT	1974-96 Leicester 1996-01 Birmingham/Nottingham/ Peterborough
UU*	1926-65 London CC 1965-74 Greater London	999 HUU	1974-97 London Central 1997-01 Wimbledon
UV*	1926-65 London CC 1965-74 Greater London	999 HUV	ditto
UW*	1926-65 London CC 1965-74 Greater London	999 HUW	ditto
UX*	1924-74 Shropshire CC	YUX 999	Shrewsbury
UY*	1924-74 Worcestershire CC	999 MUY	Worcester
UZ	1955-74 Belfast CBC	9999 UZ	Belfast
V	Lanark CC	V 9999	
VA*	1921-74 Lanark CC	999 KVA	1970-84 Cambridge 1984-01 Peterborough
VB*	1926-65 Croydon CBC 1965-74 Greater London	9999 VB 999 DVB	1974-81 Canterbury 1981-01 Maidstone (code not used)
VC*	1926-74 Coventry CBC	9999 VC 999 AVC	1974-96 Coventry 1996-01 Birmingham/ Northampton/Worcester
VD*	1928-74 Lanark CC	166 KVD	Luton (Not used after 1977)
VE*	1926-65 Cambridgeshire CC 1965-74 Cambridgeshire & Isle of Ely CC	714 EVE	1970-84 Cambridge 1984-01 Peterborough

VF*	1926-74 Norfolk CC	9999 VF 999 DVF	Norwich
VG*	1926-74 Norwich CBC	YVG 387	ditto
VH*	1926-74 Huddersfield CBC	YVH 999	1974-94 Huddersfield 1994-01 Leeds
VJ*	1926-74 Herefordshire CC	439 EVJ	1974-81 Hereford 1981-97 Gloucester 1987-01 Bristol & Worcester
VK*	1926-74 Newcastle upon Tyne CBC	999 WVK	Newcastle upon Tyne
VL*	1926-74 Lincoln CBC	XVL 387	Lincoln
VM*	1926-74 Manchester CBC	9999 VM	Manchester
VN*	1926-74 Yorkshire – North Riding CC	999 HVJ	1974-00 Middlesbrough 2000-01 Stockton@
VO	1926-74 Nottinghamshire CC	460 YVO	Nottingham
VP*	1926-74 Birmingham CBC	999 DVP	Birmingham
VR*	1928-74 Manchester CBC	9999 VR	Manchester
VS*	Greenock BC	EVS 816	Luton
VT	1926-74 Stoke-on-Trent BC	999 YVT 9999 VT	1974-96 Stoke 1996-01 Birmingham/Shrewsbury
VU*	1928-74 Manchester CBC	9999 VU	Manchester
VV*	1928-74 Northampton CBC	TVV 970	Northampton
VW	1926-74 Essex CC	999 YVW 9999 VW	Chelmsford
VX	ditto	999 YVX 9999 VX	ditto
VY*	1926-74 York CBC	2751 VY 574 BVY	1974-80 York 1980-01 Leeds
VZ	1956-74 Tyrone CC	9999 VZ	Omagh
W	Sheffield CBC	9999 W	
WA	1919-74 Sheffield CBC	9999 WA 999 JWA	Sheffield
WB	1921-74 Sheffield CBC	9999 WB 999 JWB	ditto
WC	1961-74 Essex CC	999 YWC	Chelmsford
WD	1928-74 Warwickshire CC	9999 WD 999 KWD	1974-93 Dudley 1993-01 Birmingham
WE	1926-74 Sheffield CBC	9999 WE 570 JWE	Sheffield
WF	1924-74 Yorkshire – East Riding CC	9999 WF 625 CWF	ditto
WG	1928-74 Stirling CC	XWG 923	ditto
WH	1924-74 Bolton CBC	YWH 992	1974-81 Bolton 1981-01 Manchester
WI	1903-86 Waterford CBC	WWI 80	
WJ	1928-74 Sheffield CBC	9999 WJ 999 HWJ	Sheffield
WK	1924-74 Coventry CBC	8511 WK 702 CWK	1974-96 Coventry 1996-01 Birmingham/ Northampton/Worcester
WL	1924-72 Oxford CBC 1972-74 Oxford CBC and Oxfordshire CC	999 VWL	Oxford

WM	1924-74 Southport CBC	YWM 999	1974-96 Liverpool 1996-01 Not used
WN	1924-74 Swansea CBC	368 JWM	Swansea
WO	1924-74 Monmouth CC	999 JWO	Cardiff
WP	1928-74 Worcestershire CC	999 MWP	Worcester
WR	1915-74 Yorkshire – West Riding CC	999 HWR	Leeds
WS	1903-20 Leith BC 1920-74 Edinburgh BC	YWS 999	Edinburgh
WT	1922-74 Yorkshire – West Riding CC	633 HWT	Leeds
WU	1923-74 Yorkshire – West Riding CC	9999 WU 999 CWU	ditto
WV	1928-74 Wiltshire CC	998 EWV	Brighton
WW	1924-74 Yorkshire – West Riding CC	9999 WW 999 CWW	Leeds
WX	1926-74 Yorkshire – West Riding CC	9999 WX 999 CWX	ditto
WY	1921-74 Yorkshire – West Riding CC	9999 WY 999 CWY	ditto
WZ	1956-74 Belfast CBC	9999 WZ	Belfast
X	Northumberland CC	X 9999	
XA*	1920-63 London CC 1963-74 Kirkcaldy BC	999 GXA	
XB*	1920-63 London CC 1964-74 Coatbridge BC	999 GXB	
XC*	1920-63 London CC 1964-74 Solihull CBC	999 GXC	
XD*	1920-63 London CC 1964-74 Luton CBC	999 GXD	
XE*	1920-63 London CC 1964-74 Luton CBC	999 GXE	
XF*	1920-63 London CC 1968-74 Torbay CBC	999 GXF	
XG*	1928-68 Middlesbrough CBC 1968-74 Teesside CBC	SXG 998	
XH*	1920-63 London CC	999 GXH	
XI	1921-74 Belfast CBC	9999 XI	Belfast
XJ*	1930-74 Manchester CBC	6057 XJ	Manchester
XK*	1921-63 London CC	999 GXK	
XL*	ditto	999 GXL	
XM*	ditto	999 GXM	
XN*	ditto	999 GXN	
XO*	ditto	999 GXO	
XP*	ditto	999 GXP	1993-01 Used for tax-free exports to EC (see chapter 10)
XR*	ditto	999 GXR	
XS*	Paisley BC	JXS 692	
XT*	1923-63 London CC	999 GXT	
XU*	ditto	999 GXU	
XV*	ditto	999 GXV	
XW*	ditto	999 GXW	
XX*	1924-63 London CC	999 GXX	

XY*	ditto	999 GXY	
XZ	1957-74 Armagh CC	9999 XZ In use	Armagh
Y	Somerset CC	Y 9999	
YA	1921-74 Somerset CC	999 YYA	1974-96 Taunton 1996/01 Bristol/Exeter
YB	1923-74 Somerset CC	999 YYB	ditto
YC	1924-74 Somerset CC	896 YYC	ditto
YD	1928-74 Somerset CC	1 YYD	ditto
YE*	1926-65 London CC 1965-74 Greater London	999 HYE	ditto
YF*	ditto	999 HYF	ditto
YG*	1928-74 Yorkshire – West Riding CC	999 GYG	Leeds
YH*	1926-65 London CC 1965-74 Greater London	999 HYH	1974-97 London Central 1997-01 Wimbledon
YI	1921-52 Dublin CBC 1952-86 Dublin CC & Dublin CBC	9999 YI 999 YYI	
YJ*	1930-74 Dundee BC	RYJ 999	Brighton
YK*	1924-65 London CC 1965-74 Greater London	999 HYK	1974-97 London Central 1997-01 Wimbledon
YL*	ditto	999 HYL	ditto
YM*	ditto	798 HYM	ditto
YN*	ditto	887 HYN	ditto
YO*	ditto	999 HYO	ditto
YP*	ditto	999 HYP	ditto
YR*	ditto	999 HYR	ditto
YS*	1903-12 Partick BC 1912-74 Glasgow BC	999 JYS	Glasgow
YT*	1926-65 London CC 1965-74 Greater London	999 HYT	1974-97 London Central 1997-01 Wimbledon
YU*	ditto	999 HYU	ditto
YV*	ditto	999 HYV	ditto
YW*	ditto	999 HYW	ditto
YX*	ditto	999 HYX	ditto
YY*	ditto	999 HYY	ditto
YZ	1957-74 Londonderry CC	9999 YZ In use	Coleraine
Z	1926-52 Dublin CC 1952-86 Dublin CC & Dublin CBC	9999 Z	
ZA	1932-52 Dublin CBC 1952-86 Dublin CC & Dublin CBC	9999 ZA 999 YZA	
ZB	1932-74 Cork CC 1974-86 Cork CC & Cork CBC	YZB 999	
ZC	1937-52 Dublin CBC 1952-86 Dublin CC & Dublin CBC	9999 ZC 999 YZC	
ZD	1939-52 Dublin CBC 1952-86 Dublin CC & Dublin CBC	9999 ZD 999 YZD	

ZE	Ditto	9999 ZE 999 YZE	
ZF	1946-74 Cork CBC 1974-86 Cork CC & Cork CBC	9999 ZF 542 FZF	
ZG	1981-86 Dublin CC & Dublin CBC	YZG 999	
ZH	1947-52 Dublin CBC 1952-86 Dublin CC & Dublin CBC	9999 ZH 999 YZH	
ZI	1926-52 Dublin CBC 1952-86 Dublin CC & Dublin CBC	9999 ZI 999 YZI	
ZJ	1948-52 Dublin CBC 1952-86 Dublin CC & Dublin CBC	9999 ZJ 999 YZJ	
ZK	1949-74 Cork CC 1974-86 Cork CC & Cork CBC	9999 ZK 999 YZK	
ZL	1950-52 Dublin CBC 1952-86 Dublin CC & Dublin CBC	9999 ZL 999 YZL	
ZM	1950-86 Galway CC	9999 ZM 779 GZM	
ZN	1951-86 Meath CC	88 ZN	
ZO	1951-86 Dublin CC & Dublin CBC	9999 ZO 999 YZO	
ZP	1951-86 Donegal CC	4853 ZP	
ZR	1951-86 Wexford CC	8071 ZR	
ZS	1981-86 Dublin CC & Dublin CBC	ZS 8709	
ZT	1953-74 Cork CC 1974-86 Cork CC & Cork CBC	9999 ZT	
ZU	1953-86 Dublin CC & Dublin CBC	9999 ZU 999 YZU	
ZV	1981-86 Dublin CC & Dublin CBC	YZV 999 (ZV **** not issued)	From 1992, ZV **** (and subsequently ZV *****) used for vehicles over 30 years old
ZW	1953-86 Kildare CC	9343 ZW	
ZX	1953-86 Kerry CC	9999 ZX	
ZY	1954-86 Louth CC	2507 ZY	
ZZ	1925 onwards issued by various organisations and motoring clubs to vehicles temporarily imported		

+ Officially the County of Southampton until 1959.
@ These are offices which relocated rather than ones which closed.
# Officially Salop.
& Change of authority name.
% From 1971 (J-prefix) SCY issued by Cornwall (Truro after 1974) for use on Isles of Scilly.
$ Reversed ASR not issued.

APPENDIX 3 – LOCAL OFFICES: USUAL ORDER OF ISSUE (POST 2001)

Peterborough – AE, AF, AK, AJ, AD, AG, AM, AC, AA, AB, AN
Norwich – AU, AO, AP, AR, AT
Ipswich – AY, AV, AX, AW
Birmingham – BX, BU, BV, BF, BN, BK, BJ, BG, BD, BT, BL, BP, BW, BC, BA, BM
Cardiff – CN, CE, CK, CA, CF, CJ
Swansea – CU, CV, CP, CT, CR
Bangor – CX, CW (CY from 06)
Chester – DK, DG, DE, DA, DF, DC, DH
Shrewsbury – DX, DU, DY, DV, DN, DS, DL, DP, DT, DW
Chelmsford – EU, EY, EX, EO, EK, EA, EJ, EF, EN, ET, EG, EP, EW
Nottingham – FJ, FN, FE, FL, FG, FP, FD, FH, FM, FA, FB, FC, FF
Lincoln – FX, FY, FV, FT, FR, FW
Maidstone – GN, GK GJ, GF, GL, GD, GM, GC, GH
Brighton – GX, GU, GY, GV, GP, GR, GW
Bournemouth – HF, HJ. HG, HD, HC
Portsmouth – HX, HY, HV, HN, HK, HT, HS, HL (HW - Isle of Wight)
Luton (to 2008) – KE, KF, KJ, KL, KG, KD. KC. KH, KB, KA, KK
Northampton – KX, KY, KU, KV, KN, KP, KM, KR, KS, KW, KT, KO
Northampton (08 onwards) – KX, KY, KU, KV, KN, KP, KM, KR, KS, KW, KT, KO, KJ, KK
Wimbledon – LJ, LF, LG, LD, LC, LB, LA, LE, LH
Stanmore/Borehamwood – LK, LN, LT, LR, LS, LM, LL, LO, LP
Stanmore/Borehamwood (08 onwards) – LK, LN, LT, LR, LS, LM, LL, LO, LP, KE, KF, KD, KC
Sidcup – LX, LV. LY, LW, LU
Manchester – MX, MV, MK, MF.MA. ML, MJ, MT, MW, MM, MD, MC, MH, MP, MB, ME
Newcastle – NK, NJ, NL, NA, ND, NG, NC, NH, NM, NB, NE
Stockton – NX, NU, NV, NY, NT, NR
Oxford – OU, OY, OV, OE, OW, OX
Preston – PO, PN, PE, PK, PJ, PF, PL, PG, PA, PM
Kendal – PX, PY, PV
Reading/Theale – RX, RK, RV, RO RE, RJ, RF, RA, RY, RN, RL, RD, RG
Glasgow – SF, SJ, SG, SA, SD, SH, SB, SC
Edinburgh – SN SK SL SM SO
Dundee – SP, ST, SR, SS
Aberdeen – SV, SW
Inverness – SY, SX
Worcester – VX, VU. VO. VK. VN. VR, VS
Exeter – WA, WJ, WF, WG, WD, WH
Truro – WK, WL
Bristol – WX, WU, WV, WN, WR, WP, WM, WO, WT
Leeds – YJ, YK, YD, YG, TH, YE, YF, YB, YA, YL
Sheffield – YN, YT, YR, YP, YS, YM, YO, YU, YV
Beverley – YX, YY, YW

APPENDIX 4 – AGE IDENTIFIERS

	Start	End
	Suffix Letters	
A	18 February 1963	31 December 1963
B	1 January 1964	31 December 1964
C	1 January 1965	31 December 1965
D	1 January 1966	31 December 1966
E	1 January 1967	31 July 1967
F	1 August 1967	31 July 1968
G	1 August 1968	31 July 1969
H	1 August 1969	31 July 1970
J	1 August 1970	31 July 1971
K	1 August 1971	31 July 1972
L	1 August 1972	31 July 1973
M	1 August 1973	31 July 1974
N	1 August 1974	31 July 1975
P	1 August 1975	31 July 1976
R	1 August 1976	31 July 1977
S	1 August 1977	31 July 1978
T	1 August 1978	31 July 1979
V	1 August 1979	31 July 1980
W	1 August 1980	31 July 1981
X	1 August 1981	31 July 1982
Y	1 August 1982	31 July 1983
	Prefix Letters	
A	1 August 1983	31 July 1984
B	1 August 1984	31 July 1985
C	1 August 1985	31 July 1986
D	1 August 1986	31 July 1987
E	1 August 1987	31 July 1988
F	1 August 1988	31 July 1989
G	1 August 1989	31 July 1990
H	1 August 1990	31 July 1991
J	1 August 1991	31 July 1992
K	1 August 1992	31 July 1993
L	1 August 1993	31 July 1994
M	1 August 1994	31 July 1995
N	1 August 1995	31 July 1996
P	1 August 1996	31 July 1997
R	1 August 1997	31 July 1998
S	1 August 1998	28 February 1999
T	1 March 1999	31 August 1999
V	1 September 1999	29 February 2000

	Start	End
W	1 March 2000	31 August 2000
X	1 September 1999	28 February 2001
Y	1 March 2001	31 August 2001
	Current System	
51	1 September 2001	28 February 2002
02	1 March 2002	31 August 2002
52	1 September 2002	28 February 2003
03	1 March 2003	31 August 2002
53	1 September 2003	29 February 2004
04	1 March 2004	31 August 2004
54	1 September 2004	28 February 2005
05	1 March 2005	31 August 2005
55	1 September 2005	28 February 2006
06	1 March 2006	31 August 2006
56	1 September 2006	28 February 2007
07	1 March 2007	31 August 2007
57	1 September 2007	29 February 2008
08	1 March 2008	31 August 2008
58	1 September 2008	28 February 2009
09	1 March 2009	31 August 2009
59	1 September 2009	28 February 2010
10	1 March 2010	31 August 2010
60	1 September 2010	28 February 2011
11	1 March 2011	31 August 2011
61	1 September 2011	29 February 2012
12	1 March 2012	31 August 2012
62	1 September 2012	28 February 2013
13	1 March 2013	31 August 2013
63	1 September 2013	28 February 2014
14	1 March 2014	31 August 2014
64	1 September 2014	28 February 2015
15	1 March 2015	31 August 2015
65	1 September 2015	28 February 2015
16	1 March 2016	31 August 2016
66	1 September 2016	29 February 2016
17	1 March 2017	31 August 2017
67	1 September 2017	28 February 2018
18	1 March 2018	31 August 2018
68	1 September 2018	28 February 2019
19	1 March 2019	31 August 2019
69	1 September 2019	28 February 2020
70	1 March 2020	31 August 2020

APPENDIX 5 – IRISH REPUBLIC CODES FROM 1987

C – Cork
CE – Clare
CN - Cavan
CW – Carlow

D – Dublin
DL – Donegal

G – Galway

KE – Kildare
KK – Kilkenny

L (from 2014) – Limerick City and County
L (to 2013) – Limerick County
LD – Longford
LH – Louth
LK (to 2013) – Limerick City
LM – Leitrim
LS – Laois

MH – Meath
MN – Monaghan
MO – Mayo

OY – Offaly

RN – Roscommon

SO – Sligo

T (from 2014) – Tipperary
TN (to 2014) – Tipperary North Riding
TS (to 2014) – Tipperary South Riding

W (from 2014) – Waterford City and County
W (to 2013) – Waterford County
WD (to 2013) – Waterford City
WH – Westmeath
WW – Wicklow
WX - Wexford

INDEX

As this book explains, there was a major change in how registrations were issued in 1974. Before 1974 they were issued by local authorities, afterwards by Local Vehicle Licensing Offices (LVLO), subsequently called Vehicle Registration Offices and finally Local Offices. Many LVLOs were established in towns which had been registration authorities, e.g. Bolton and Bristol. In compiling this index I have felt it necessary to differentiate between references to local authorities and LVLOs. To resolve these issues and to use Bolton as an example, the entry "Bolton" refers to the local authority and "Bolton LO" refers to the LVLO. The Bolton LVLO was actually closed before its title was changed to "Vehicle Registration Office" and then "Local Office", but for simplicity's state I have just used "LO" to describe all post-1974 offices, even if they closed before the "Local Office" title was adopted.

Durham LO: 40

East Ham: 31
East Lothian: 32
Eastbourne: 13, 15
Eastwood: 77
Edinburgh: 9, 17, 39, 77
Elginshire: 9
Ely, Isle of: 12, 16, 32
Enfield: 75
Enniskillen LO: 58
Essex: 16, 29, 31, 39, 75
Estate car: 81
Ethiopia: 72
Europlate: 119
Eurosymbol: 52, 60, 114

Fermanagh: 58
Firmin, Alan: 82
Ford: 46
France: 114

Galway: 59
Germany: 114
Glamorganshire: 23, 32
Glasgow: 9, 16, 17, 24, 76, 77, 96
Glasgow LO: 50
Gloucester: 96
Gloucester LO: 46
Gloucestershire: 9, 10, 96
Goods vehicles: 81, 82
Govan: 17
Great Britain: 114
Greece: 114
Greenock: 32, 39, 77
Greyhound Racing Association: 24
Grimsby LO: 40
Guildford LO: 46

Hampshire: 20, 96

Hanley: 12, 16
Harrods: 11
Hartlepool: 32
Hastings: 11, 75
Hastings LO: 40
Haverfordwest LO: 41, 46
Heinz: 43
Hereford LO: 40
Hertfordshire: 16, 24, 32, 39
Holland – see Nederland
HP Information Ltd: 33
Huddersfield: 31
Huddersfield LO: 46
Hull – see Kingston upon Hull
Hull LO: 47
Humber: 96
Hungary: 114
Huntingdon: 32
Hyphen: 8

Ilford LO: 46, 47
India: 73
International Cocoa Organization: 74
International Maritime Organization: 72
Inverness: 36
Ipswich: 21, 32
Ireland: 8, 9, 16, 42, 50, 73, 106
Israel: 73
Italy: 73, 114

Johnson, Amy: 17, 24
Jordan: 72

Kahn, Afzal: 75
Kavanagh, JJ Ltd: 61
Keith LO: 40
Kendal LO: 40
Kent: 15, 16, 23, 96
Kings County: 9, 59

Kingston upon Hull: 16, 96
Kirkcaldy: 31, 75, 97, 98
Kirkwall LO: 40
Kithead Trust: 37, 121

Lancashire: 28, 31, 38
Lanarkshire: 9, 77
Laoighis: 9, 59
Leeds: 96
Leicester: 21, 75
Leicester LO: 46
Leith: 12, 17
Lerwick LO: 40
Limerick: 61
Lindsey: 14
Liverpool: 15, 16, 26, 37, 96
Liverpool LO: 39, 46
Local Government Board: 8, 14, 17, 78
Logbook: 18
London-Brighton Run: 68
London Central LO: 46, 47, 63
London, City of: 77
London CC: 14, 15, 22, 23, 24, 31, 37, 63, 65, 96
London, Greater London Council: 31, 35, 63
London Midland & Scottish Railway Co: 24
London NE LO: 46, 47
London NW LO: 46
London SE LO: 46, 47
London SW LO: 46, 47
Luton: 31, 98
Luton LO: 39, 49

Malaysia: 72
Malta: 106
Man, Isle of: 16, 29, 40

Manchester: 37, 96
Manchester LO: 50
Maurice, Jack: 86
Merioneth: 12
Merthyr Tydfil: 15
Metropolitan Police: 22
MG: 7
Middlesbrough: 32
Middlesbrough LO: 47
Middlesex: 15, 17, 22,
24, 25, 26, 28, 29, 30,
31, 37, 101
Midlothian: 77, 96
Miller, Sir James: 77
Monaco: 114
Montenegro: 114
Morayshire: 9
Motherwell and
Wishaw: 17, 31
Motor Union: 78
Motorcycles: 19, 20,
21, 27, 31, 39, 52, 84,
98

Napier: 10
Nederland: 72, 114
New Zealand: 72
Newcastle: 75
Newport LO: 40
Nigeria: 72
Norfolk: 12, 16, 98
Northampton: 10, 15
Northampton LO: 47
Northamptonshire: 16
Northumberland: 16,
21, 31, 32
Nottingham: 96

Oban LO: 40
Offaly: 9, 59
Oldham: 12
Oman: 72
Orkney: 68
Overland: 95
Oxford: 16, 31, 32
Oxford LO: 50

Oxfordshire: 32, 67

Pakistan: 73
Pankhurst, Christabel:
12
Papua New Guinea: 73
Partick: 17
Peebles: 68
Perth: 39
Peterborough LO: 39
Peterborough, Soke of:
32
Plymouth: 16, 17, 31
Plymouth LO: 40
Popemobile: 61
Portsmouth LO: 40, 42
Portugal: 114
Post Office: 23
Preston LO: 50
Public Carriage Office:
9

Qatar: 73
Quebec: 73
Queens County: 9, 59
Queensland: 73

Reading: 16, 32
Reading LO: 38, 41, 55
Register a Vehicle: 55
Regn Newsletter: 119
Regn Nos Club: 119
Renfrewshire: 11, 76
Road Research
Laboratory: 34
Rolls-Royce: 97
Ross and Cromarty: 36
RAF: 71
RAF Mildenhall:
Royal Automobile Club:
63
Royal Irish Automobile
Club: 62
Royal Irish
Constabulary: 48

Royal Scottish
Automobile Club: 63
Ruislip LO: 46
Rumania: 114
Russell, Earl: 7, 10, 11
Russia: 114
Rutland: 68
Rye, Claude: 24

St Boswells LO: 40
St Helens: 38
St Vincent: 72
Salford: 31, 96
Salisbury LO: 40
Scilly, Isles: 35
Scotland: 8, 9, 16, 39,
50, 54, 55
Second World War: 24
Selkirk LO: 40
Servia: 114
Sheffield LO: 54
Sidcup LO: 46, 47
Smethwick: 15, 32, 76
Solihull: 31, 75, 98
Somerset: 11, 28, 96
Southend: 15, 39, 75
Southport: 14
Spain: 72, 106, 113
Staffordshire: 10, 13,
18, 20, 25, 26, 29, 30,
31, 34
Stanmore LO: 46, 55
Stewart and Arden: 17,
24
Stockport: 11, 31, 95
Stockton LO: 47
Stoke-on-Trent: 12, 16,
76
Stoke LO: 46
Stornoway LO: 36, 40
Straits Settlements:
114
Stranraer LO: 40
Suffolk, East: 32
Surrey: 22, 28, 96